CONSCIOUS GRIEF

CONSCIOUS GRIEF

TRANSFORMING PAIN INTO EVOLUTION AND GROWTH

TARA NASH

MANUSCRIPTS
PRESS

CONSCIOUS GRIEF

Transforming Pain into Evolution and Growth

ISBN   979-8-88926-544-3   *Paperback*
979-8-88926-545-0   *Ebook*

For my parents, Penny and Peter.

Thank you for bringing me into this world and for guiding and inspiring me in everything I do.

Contents

The most beautiful people we have known are those who have known defeat, known suffering, known struggle, known loss, and have found their way out of the depths. These persons have an appreciation, a sensitivity, and an understanding of life that fills them with compassion, gentleness, and a deep loving concern. Beautiful people do not just happen.

—ELISABETH KÜBLER-ROSS

INTRODUCTION

"I think you should base your second-year project on the death of your father," Paula Majeski said.

Why? I thought.

I was meeting with Paula, facilitator of Healing Consciousness, when working toward a degree at the University of Santa Monica. Her suggestion had totally shocked me. I walked away from our meeting thinking, I wish I had not gone to see that woman. Does she want me to be miserable the entire year?

Other people were learning to pole dance as a basis for their projects! Why couldn't I do something that fun?

I had no idea when I embarked on a Spiritual Psychology Masters in Los Angeles in 2014 that death and grieving would become my focus. My original idea for my second-year project was to do a business plan for a restaurant concept called Café Conscious.

However, three separate friends had suggested I speak with Paula Majeski, so I sought her out.

After that conversation, I let the information gestate for a few days. I was living in the dreamy hills of Topanga Canyon, a serene, beautiful place where my soul could listen. Looking out from my living room at the rolling ridges and beautiful sunsets, I ruminated on the curriculum I was studying. After a few days, the awareness dropped in. I always want to talk about death, but no one else does. Perhaps this could be a really interesting project?

What I initially thought of as a miserable topic became a profoundly deep and touching process. As bizarre as it may sound, I came to find the subject of death and grief lit me up. For as long as I can remember, I have yearned to have deep conversations and connect with like-minded people who shared similar stories to mine.

To start the project, I posted a message on my Facebook page asking if people would be open to sharing their experiences of loss with me. I interviewed friends and acquaintances and discovered that some people had never shared their stories before.

Why is this? I wondered.

The most profound experiences in our lives are not always given the space they so richly deserve. We are pushed to move on quickly. Empty platitudes try and smooth over the rough and jagged edges of one of life's hardest lessons. I had initially rejected the idea of focusing on my father's death for my thesis because it sounded depressing. My impulse was to veer to something lighter. I wanted to avoid thinking about the loss of my father, as well as that of my mother. I had done this my entire life, believing most people—myself included—want to be around upbeat, sunny-side up Tara!

During that year, my conscious grieving began. I finally gave myself permission to mourn. I talked about my dead parents and remembered them. I honored the deep well of pain, not as something to avoid but as something to lean into and excavate. I read books about grief, I wrote about the feelings that were being revealed, and I did spiritual practices communicating with my dead parents. I had my first reading with a medium—which turned out to be a profound conversation with my parents—with a good dose of joking and humor. I began to facilitate grief groups as a volunteer for a charity called Our House.

I discovered Death Cafés and sighed internally; of course this exists in California! I researched these self-run groups founded specifically for weirdos like myself who wanted to talk about death when no one else did! I was bowled over to discover that this movement was founded by a fellow Brit in Primrose Hill, only a few short miles from my home in Notting Hill, West London. I began to find my tribe, my heart beating that little bit faster every time I made a discovery that resonated.

I had been unconsciously grieving for almost my whole life, but I had very little understanding of what grief was. I thought it was feeling sad and that it lasted for a short time after someone died. Then, in my early twenties, uncontrollable emotions started ricocheting through me after my mother died. I did not relate it back to her death or to that of my father so many years before her.

I was nine years old in 1990 when my father died suddenly. The mourning period was short-lived. We had his funeral and life moved on. My mother remarried quickly and threw herself into work. I never saw her grieve. In an effort to survive, she did what she thought was best. Her grandmother's words "You are still young enough to find a new husband" propelled her in this direction. Unfortunately, her marriage quickly turned toxic. She divorced after three years—more grief. Later the family business had to be sold—more grief. Her attempts at finding another long-lasting loving relationship never happened—more grief. At the age of fifty-five, she was diagnosed with breast cancer, and at fifty-seven, she passed. Grief echoed throughout the family and in turn buried itself deep within.

I am certain that if my mother were still here, she would agree that her pain went unprocessed. I cannot help but wonder if things would have worked out differently had she taken the time to grieve consciously.

In the years between the deaths of my father and mother, I had grandparents and pets who died. I had to make the decision to have my horse put down. I witnessed my mother's divorce and saying goodbye to another father figure. I had secondary losses. I lost my mother to her career, I grew up quickly, and I grieved the loss of my innocence and my childhood.

I was twenty-one when my mother died, and I pretty much replicated what she had shown me. I stayed busy as I attempted to fill the void. I often questioned my existence. Life felt arduous. When my father died, I made the decision to not show emotions. Everyone was so sad and shocked; I didn't want to add to the pain by showing mine. I became numb—numb to the bad and to the good.

This is how trauma can impact us.

I carried so much unconscious grief, desperate to be felt and nurtured, but I kept running from it and blaming other parts of my life. I spent years building walls around my heart to protect myself. Life felt like one painful event after the other. I decided to armor up to avoid any more pain. Now, as I look back, I feel annoyed that no one sat me down and explained what grief was and how it could impact me as it lurked in the sidelines. For this reason, I am compelled to write this book and share what I have learned. From my experience and the experience of others, I hope to help people navigate this often confusing, conflicting, and misunderstood process of grief and mourning.

Through conscious grieving, I found the closer I got to my pain, the more engaged I felt with my life. For so long, I had repressed emotions and tried to explain away my issues by blaming them on other circumstances in my life. I did that because grief is really hard and my ego was trying to divert me from feeling the most painful things in my past. I honestly felt that if I started to cry, I would never stop. It brings me to tears just to write that because, yes, pain lives inside me and my grief will always be there, and that is okay. I am not afraid of it anymore. I embrace it, because my heart feels soft and open where it was once cold and closed in fear.

The good news is that through conscious grieving, my life changed.

I now feel more joy, love, and excitement than I ever did before. I am grateful for my human life after spending many years not caring if I was here or not. For a time in the past, I wanted to isolate from my sisters, my only family. At Christmas in 2012, the thought of being with them felt too challenging for me. They had their husbands and children. I was living alone in London, filling my void with food and work. I looked for an escape and ended up taking myself away to spend Christmas alone that year.

In contrast to that, since grieving consciously, I spent two years during the pandemic living with my sister Polly. I am so grateful for the home and family she has created. Home and family like this used to trigger my grief, making me want to run because it reminded me of the young life I once had. On many occasions, I would leave her house and binge heavily on food on the drive back to London. That does not happen anymore because I started to confront my pain and let it out. I made the intention to replace the hurt inside with love. Taking the time and doing the work was not the responsibility of anyone else but me.

Conscious Grief takes grit and courage; it is not easy, but it is enriching and life affirming.

We all carry grief in some form, so this book is for everyone who has ever experienced it. You may not have the time and space in your life for conscious grieving right now. Please do not feel the pressure to take it on if that is the case. Maybe you received this book as a gift from a friend who is worried that you are holding grief inside. Rest assured, your grief is unique. You will find no right or wrong way. Some parts of this book may resonate, others may not. When your consciousness is ready, your grief will be waiting to be tended to. It took me over twenty years! Remember, grief does not carry a timeline.

You might have had a recent loss and are feeling so much pain and torment in this moment that you feel like you are going crazy. Perhaps you need help with how to manage the tsunami of emotions swirling around inside you and do not know where to turn. This book will give you suggestions on how to support yourself and information on the people and places who can help. I have included a Resource Section at the back of this book with references to therapists, coaches, and communities you can reach out to.

The chapters have been sequenced to lead you in the direction of being able to integrate your grief, to make you feel whole again. That said, if you want to jump around and delve into a later chapter, that is totally fine. At the end of each chapter, I have given some prompts, which I call Heart Work. I advise getting a new journal to dedicate to your conscious grieving so you can delve deeply through the medium of writing, pen to paper. If you don't get the opportunity to buy a journal, I have left blank pages in the back of the book for Heart Work notes.

You may want to highlight and write notes on the pages within. You might read something that sparks questions. Make a note of these and stay curious.

If we choose to grieve consciously, we strive to keep our hearts open and stay receptive to life. This will lead to a more compassionate human being and, my hope is, to a more compassionate society.

By reading this book, you may relate to some of the stories from people who have experienced pain and grief when life has been cruel. They share how they moved through the grief process and what they learned. A lot of these people have transformed their pain into their life's work, helping others navigate their grief. My hope is this book unites you with your pain and that it is not something foreign or fearful but something to embrace. My hope is that you will know you are not alone.

I truly believe we are all teachers for one another and that we heal best in community. To that end, I have developed the Conscious Grief Program. The chapters here follow the basis of that course. I share my own personal experience and also weave in the touching grief stories from people in my Conscious Grief Series Interviews. My wish is that this book will be your companion in navigating your way through the rocky terrain of grief to bring joy, connection, and happiness.

Grief is like a precious ritual. When something rocks our internal world, it is up to us to treat it with the tenderness and care it deserves. Are you ready for your Conscious Grief journey to begin?

AWARENESS

CHAPTER 1

Grief Consciousness

"A terrible disconnect exists between what the average person thinks grief should look and feel like—typically, a series of progressive, time-limited stages that end in a state of 'closure'—and how grief, that artful dodger, actually behaves" (Edelman 2020, xvi).

Grief is hard. It hurts. It exhausts us. It torments us. It is hard to talk about because we are not always equipped to put the devastation and intense loss and sadness into words.

Sometimes we feel we have no one to turn to. It can make us want to isolate because nobody can identify with the inner turmoil.

In the immediate response of shock and disbelief, a numbness can occur. We might get stuck there. If we become accustomed to numbing, we are incapable of being in touch with our feelings. We bottle them up, screw the lid on tightly, and let the pressure build.

If you are in touch with your feelings, it can be a scary thing because there is an overwhelming intensity of emotions that haven't been felt before.

Some feelings we might judge as unacceptable. So, we keep them a secret and hope they disappear.

GRIEF DEFINED

"Grief—Intense sorrow, especially caused by someone's death" (Oxford Language Dictionary 2006).

"Grief is the normal and natural reaction to loss of any kind" (James and Friedman 2009).

Grief is felt when someone dies, but grief is experienced in all types of loss and change.

We don't acknowledge grief often enough.

WHY IS THIS?

To understand our cultural dismissal of grief, we need to look back in history. I am born and raised in the UK. When I refer to my cultural understanding of grief, it is from this vantage point.

I was honored to interview best-selling author Hope Edelman in my first Conscious Grief Series. During our conversation, we discussed her most recent book The After Grief: Finding Your Way on the Long Path of Loss, which starts by outlining the history of grief. Hope said, "If we think about the nineteenth century, the Victorian era, the Romantics, they were very much in touch with their grief, they had elaborate and intricate rituals for mourning the death of a loved one, it was a very social experience and highly emotional. In fact, the romantics believed if you did not outwardly show your distress then perhaps you had not really loved that person who had died."

After this, major shifts in the world altered the way people grieved. Mass casualties from World War I meant men were buried on the battlefields. This was followed with the 1918–1920 flu pandemic, culminating in so much death it simply was not possible to have elaborate funerals and mourn multiple losses in the way they had done before.

Edelman notes the work of British sociologist and historian Tony Walter. Walter writes about the uprising of the suffragettes who rose up against the rituals of mourning. Women were the ones required to change their clothes and stay at home, while men carried on with life as normal. Women thought this was unfair (Edelman 2020).

Dead people were laid in state in their homes, and bodies were prepared for burial by their family. Then death was moved from the home and outsourced to hospitals and funeral homes. Increasingly, people became detached from death.

Edelman writes about Sigmund Freud's Mourning and Melancholia, written in 1915. Freud lays out that grief is an internal experience and came up with the idea that successful mourning "was achieved only after an individual fully relinquished all emotional and psychic attachments to the lost object and reinvested that energy in a new relationship" (Freud 2015).

Freud's theory gathered momentum; it was the perfect pairing for the Industrial Revolution. Efficiency became everything, and this idea meant people could return to work quickly. The resounding message was Get over it and move on.

Shortly after the publication, Freud's daughter Sophie died, followed by her young son. Freud now knew deep personal grief and found no successful mourning solution. However, his initial theory was widely known and used by academics and healthcare clinicians.

The UK pioneered capitalism with the Industrial Revolution; it is no wonder that we adopted the stiff upper lip. Given this history, it makes sense that we are grief illiterate and find it hard to express and talk about emotions.

You might have heard of the "Five Stages of Grief" by Elisabeth Kübler-Ross. This widely known model was created when Kübler-Ross observed people who were dying. The stages are anger, bargaining, depression, and acceptance as they moved toward death (Kübler-Ross 1969). This has become a contentious model, criticized for being a linear process. Kübler-Ross never meant for it to be used for those who were grieving.

Like with Freud's findings, it gave health care professionals and academics something to grasp about a process that is complex and hard to quantify. We like to categorize and organize, as if somehow doing this gives us a sense of control over the uncontrollable.

YOUR GRIEF

If you are grieving now, I am sure you can identify with those stages and a plethora of other feelings and emotions within. I don't want to laden you with theories.

I imagine you have picked up this book because you are looking for answers, support, and assistance. Maybe you feel like you are failing at grief because it is lasting a really long time and you feel stuck. Perhaps you are suffering in silence and longing for some peace in your heart.

In our world of duality thinking, we constantly analyze: am I getting this grief thing right or wrong?

Let me confirm, there is no right or wrong way to grieve. Your grief is as unique as your fingerprint. It will not feel the same as anyone else's.

For example, my sisters and I both had the same parents who died, but our grief is completely different. Avoid comparing your grief to someone else's. Your grief alone is exhausting; you have enough to manage.

Notice if you are resisting the discomfort of strained and difficult feelings. Other people don't like seeing you in pain. It makes them uncomfortable, and they don't know what to say. People's natural response is to rush in with solutions in an attempt to fix things. Does that feel helpful?

We try to rationalize it, and we want to think our way out of it or push it aside with distractions. Grief isn't fun. It's messy, it's uncontrollable, it's inefficient, and in our busy, overstimulated lives, we feel like we don't have time for it.

HOW MY GRIEF BEGAN IN 1990

My unconscious grief started when my father died. Moments from the morning after it happened are still firmly etched in my mind. I woke up and heard my mother in my elder sister's bedroom. Lisa was crying, and I thought they were in an argument. I asked, "What are you arguing about now?" My mother, sitting on the side of Lisa's bed, turned and gently said to me, "We're not arguing, darling. Daddy died last night! Go downstairs and see your grandparents."

I ran downstairs to find my nanny and grandad waiting for me, and I ran into their arms. But their comfort was fleeting. That fateful morning changed everything. Soon, our kitchen overflowed with distraught family and friends grieving the unexpected death of our father. Grown adults all around me were crying and devastated. An adult male cousin just a couple years senior to my father sat at our wooden kitchen table, and what he did next left me with a lasting impression. He suddenly let out a hysterical, loud, carnal cry. He started to hyperventilate and sob. I remember he lifted his glasses to rub his eyes, as if smearing the tears would somehow ease his pain.

I cowered and ran to hide in the freezer room cupboard at the end of the kitchen. I thought, This is too much. This is so horrible to witness. In that moment, I froze. I thought, I am not going to let this affect me in the same way! Little nine-year-old Tara made the decision to be brave and strong; I would never show my pain to anyone else because this was too much to bear. I shut down, and I kept my tears to myself.

As months passed, my concerned mother took me to therapy, but I refused to talk and only attended one session. My mum had absolutely no road map on how to cope with grief. This was pre-Internet, and the mantra our family adopted was Be brave and carry on.

I had a dead dad, and I felt strange about it. When I told people he was dead, their reactions were so uncomfortable for me that I would turn the tables and end up comforting them. Often, just to avoid the awkwardness, I lied and told people I had a dad. My sense of belonging in the world had changed.

NUMBING WAS MY COPING STRATEGY

In the first two years after my father died, my grandpa Roy and his sister, my aunty Peg, died. They both died of heart-related issues, which would now be recognized as broken heart syndrome. Without doubt, the sudden death of my father had a huge impact on them.

My mother remarried quickly after my father died. For me, having a stepfather meant I could say he was my dad. This gave me that sense of belonging I was craving. However, it was short-lived. Their marriage ended in divorce by the time I was thirteen. More grief.

When I was fourteen, my grandpa Stan died. He was my mother's father. For the first time, I heard my mother crying in her bedroom. I wrote in my diary that I felt like a hard stone, because I could not console her. I judged myself harshly for that.

We had two family dogs that died during my childhood. As I mentioned in the Introduction, my mum was diagnosed with breast cancer when I was eighteen, and at the same time, I had to make the horrendous decision to have my horse—my best friend—put down.

In 2002, the absolutely unthinkable happened—my mum died of breast cancer. She was fifty-seven, and I was twenty-one. I never imagined life could be that unfair.

My mind boggles looking back at all the loss in my childhood.

It is no wonder I built strong walls around my heart in an attempt to protect myself. I adopted numbing as my coping strategy. In my teens, I realized I lacked empathy; a hardening had occurred. I started to hate myself because I could not feel. At times, I thought about suicide. I kept thinking, What is the point of life? It is so painful! I honestly thought having children was cruel because if life is a series of losses, I surely wasn't going to project that on to another human being.

I muscled through it and used what I could to make life sweeter. I will share more as we go through the chapters of this book.

Numbing as a coping strategy worked well for twenty years, but it had an expiration date. I was depressed and unable to experience the joy and excitement of life. I lived in a fog of low-level depression, caught in cycles of bingeing: first food, then alcohol, then drugs. I was riddled with guilt and did not know what made me happy. On the outside, I had a great life. I had an exciting career in fashion. I had plenty of friends around me and a full social life. But on the inside, I felt sad, lonely, and completely exhausted by life.

That's a snapshot of my experience. Yours will be completely different because, like I said, everyone's grief is unique. In this book, I have identified areas that helped me come into wholeness and peace, which is where I hope you will also land in your own time.

TOO BUSY FOR GRIEF?

Life is demanding. Jobs, families, fast-paced modern life. Many of us simply survive on platitudes like stay busy because, quite frankly, we have no other option.

I met yoga teacher and best-selling author Emma Conally-Barklem on Instagram; I had the opportunity to interview her on Conscious Grief Series 3. Emma was raised by her mother and grandmother; they were her primary caregivers and main family. Her dear grandma died in 2012, which was a huge loss for Emma. Six years later, her mother, whom she also called her best friend, died of a rare cancer.

Emma confesses that, at this time, teaching yoga was taking her around the world on retreats and "life was really busy."

She explained that she swallowed the unhelpful narratives people say and reflected that the combination of platitudes and business delayed her grief.

When the pandemic came along and life came into stillness, this is when the grief started to have an impact. Emma hit a low point and realized she wasn't coping and needed help. After meeting with a few therapists, she found the right one who was able to see the unprocessed grief needed attention.

Grief can be delayed, pushed down, and avoided, but it will not go away. It will wait until you are prepared to deal with it consciously.

CONSCIOUS GRIEF

Conscious Grief is the emotional, mental, physical, and spiritual integration of loss, which we will explore in each chapter of this book.

Conscious Grief is a choice, and it takes a level of dedication and courage to go toward our pain. It does not mean you will accelerate through grief—it means you are aware of what you are feeling and actively finding ways to support yourself in the process.

Since 2012, I was thinking about the word conscious, and I wanted to create a community and physical place called Café Conscious. The idea stemmed from a year of sobriety, asking why London did not have more places to meet friends that did not revolve around alcohol. I imagined it to be a place where you could have authentic and meaningful conversations.

A few years later, I moved to Los Angeles and became conscious of my grief for the first time. I wanted to learn how I could live with the loss of my parents. How could I allow myself to feel the feelings, sit with them, and be present to my experience? I realized that presence was key. I became aware that Conscious Grief is a moving, growing, and developmental way of being with grief. Conscious Grief is not something to fix and get over, it is something to be respected and honored.

In Conscious Grief Series 4, I interviewed Jill Cowan, cofounder of Healing to the Max. Jill's sweet son, Max, took his own life at the age of sixteen, leaving their family devastated. Their therapist suggested they find a suicide loss support group. Initially, Jill felt unsure she could listen to other people's pain and felt resistance at the idea of joining a group. As time went on, she felt the suffering couldn't get any worse, so she decided she would go to a suicide loss support group.

Jill remembers being so angry that she had to attend a group and this was her new reality. She nearly didn't get through the door of the meeting. She was afraid of not being able to speak by the emotion choking her.

It was heartbreaking to hear how she felt her choices as a mother had led to a deadly conclusion and that all her self-esteem and confidence had been stripped away. This grief was sucking the life-force energy out of Jill. She could barely eat or drink, and her body was completely shutting down. She had cardiac arrest twice, tumors appeared in every part of her mothering body, and she had lost a lot of weight. It made my heart sink when she admitted, "I didn't feel deserving of self-care" because she carried so much guilt for her son's death.

Thankfully, Jill did walk through that door of the support group and found a tiny seed of hope that saved her life. The lady leading the meeting inspired her, the room was full of love and compassion, and that was a major turning point. Her advice to all grievers is "find a compassionate community of support."

Now Jill supports others with her program designed through the lens of narrative therapy, which she named Healing to The Max. These programs are specifically for all types of survivors of a loss by suicide. It can be family, best friends, boyfriends and girlfriends, close neighbors, teachers, or coaches. This is a deeply compassionate community with multiple support courses.

Jill wisely shares, "You make a plan to consciously grieve." I concur!

I decided to create a comparison of Conscious Grief and Unconscious Grief, which is a reflection of my experience. I was operating on the unconscious side of this information for many years. The last thing I want is for people to use this as a judgment chart. We all veer from one side to the other, depending on the situation and time in our life. Some of the points in unconscious grief are necessary for survival and personal preference on how you choose to grieve.

Conscious Grief	Unconscious Grief
Feeling the range of emotions that grief brings	Numbing uncomfortable feelings with alcohol, food, substances, busyness, work, relationships etc
Being curious about what grief is and how it is impacting your life	Taking no interest in grief and how it impacts you
Making an intention to grieve	Making no space in your life to grieve
Finding support	Isolating and keeping grief a private affair
Keeping your heart open to giving and receiving love	Closing your heart as a form on protection to avoid more pain and heartbreak
Taking time to nurture yourself through self-care	Repressing emotions and keeping them contained inside of you
Connecting to your body through movement and therapies	Ignoring signals from your body that you have stuck feelings to attend to
Seeing your loss as part of your personal and spiritual curriculum	Maintaining a position as the victim that life is happening against you
Knowing grief will change with intensity, but will always be there in some capacity	Believing that grief ends after a certain amount of time
Understanding that grief is related to all different kinds of loss	See's grief as only relating to the death of a person

TYPES OF LOSS

A specific grief might have brought you to reading this book, but have you reviewed your life for how many losses you have endured? Doing a loss inventory is important because grief will activate past griefs. It is good to have awareness of this and know this is normal.

Here is a list of different kinds of loss. Circle or tick the ones that you have experienced.

1. Moving house
2. Moving country
3. Divorce
4. Ending of a relationship or friendship
5. Death of a pet
6. Getting married
7. Becoming a parent
8. Not becoming a parent
9. Becoming sober
10. Aging
11. Sexuality
12. Identity
13. Health challenges
14. Financial changes
15. Loss of faculties, e.g., sight, hearing
16. Empty nest/children leaving home
17. Sexual trauma
18. Unavailable parents
19. Environmental changes
20. Political changes
21. Fertility problems
22. IVF failure
23. Faith
24. Abortion
25. Miscarriage
26. Stillbirth
27. Loss of innocence
28. Loss of safety

29. Loss of job
30. Retirement
31. Theft

As you gain more awareness about your losses, you are moving toward Conscious Grief. We can begin to examine more layers and types of grief that exist. Ultimately, all grief needs attention and tending to. These descriptions can give context to what we're going through. Peruse them to see what resonates. Losses can linger in the dusty little corners of ourselves until we shed some light and properly grieve them.

TYPES OF GRIEF

As we gain awareness about this nebulous thing called grief, you will learn that there are labels for different kinds of grief. Here is a list taken from Grief Educator Training by David Kessler of different kinds of grief (Kessler 2023). Peruse them and see what resonates with you.

Ambiguous—grief that is hard for other people to see, e.g., miscarriage, fertility issues, or the loss of a relationship with a family member who is still alive

Anticipatory—grief that comes before the death/ divorce/move

Collective—when we grieve as a group or a public figure dies, e.g., the pandemic or Princess Diana

Complicated—when painful emotions of loss don't improve with time and are so severe that you have trouble resuming or creating your life

Cumulative—when someone experiences multiple losses during a short period or unattended grief that builds up

Disenfranchised—any grief we judge or minimize, e.g., children leaving home, miscarriage, loss of pets

Delayed—grief we do not feel in the moment because it is not safe and we are in survival mode

Inconclusive—there is no body to grieve, there is hope, it breeds conspiracy theories

Masked—grief that is presenting in another way, and the resulting feeling is actually a response to grief, e.g., anger

Secondary Loss—the other losses that accompany grief in addition to the primary emotional response

Traumatic—combines trauma with bereavement or grief responses

I hope you now feel acquainted with grief, what it is, and why it can get delayed or processed unconsciously.

At the end of each chapter, I have included a list of questions or actions for you to consider. I invite you to journal using these prompts.

HEART WORK

- What messages about grief are you getting from society and the community around you?

- Have you had other losses in your life that you may not have grieved? What are they for you?

- Did you recognize any of the types of grief? What came up for you?

- Our natural response is finding ways to stop the pain. Can you sit with it and develop a relationship with your grief?

- Be open and curious to grief. From reading this chapter, what have you learned about grief?

- Are you ready to set an intention to grieve consciously?

CHAPTER 2

Self-Care

Self-care is defined as "the practice of taking an active role in protecting one's own well-being and happiness, in particular during periods of stress" (Oxford Language Dictionary 2006).

In desperate times, we go through phases of how we want to treat ourselves and what we believe will help us feel better or worse. The only person who can consciously make a choice in how you respond to what has happened is you. Self-care may feel at the bottom of your list of priorities. It is essential to bring this to the top of your list in times of grieving.

The first piece of advice is: **eat, breathe, sleep**. You may need someone to remind you to do these basic tasks in looking after yourself in acute stages of grief.

I want to remind you that you matter, your life matters, and you are loved. Life might feel pointless right now. Thoughts about ending your life may cross your mind. If you are consumed by these thoughts, please call a suicide help line immediately. Tell someone you are having suicidal thoughts and please do not keep this to yourself. In community, we heal. Find trusted people and professionals who can help point you in the right direction. Be courageous and ask for help.

Alternatively, you might be in shock and denial and running on adrenalin. Life is moving you forward, and you have very little time to reflect or slow down.

Growing up, I watched my mother religiously prioritize her forty-minute swimming sessions as a way of keeping fit and staying trim. This discipline and routine was in place long before she became a widow. Her diet was healthy but leaning toward the restrictive side. She was not the kind of woman who sat on the sofa with a tub of Ben & Jerry's, which is much more my style.

My mother modeled healthy choices for her outward appearance, but the inside job of feeling her grief was pushed down. She had no time for it. Instead, she threw herself into running the family business. It was like a fresh start for her, but it was also a huge distraction. Busyness was her way of coping.

While she was occupied becoming a businesswoman, I was busy looking after my pony. Since the age of five, I had been an avid rider, and every Christmas and birthday, I asked for a pony. My parents always said I would have to wait until I was ten years old. My relentless begging negotiated them down a year. I was delighted! My dad went all in and converted a garage into two small stables and a tack room. He was so supportive in helping me with Picolo, the 13.2 black gelding pony. He died only a few months later. Leaving me with Picolo was the greatest gift.

My mother was not at all into helping me because she was afraid of horses. This meant I was responsible for looking after this animal, which gave me discipline and structure as I woke up each day and attended to his needs. I loved everything about having a pony: riding, grooming, cleaning the tack, making his stable bed as perfect as I could, entering horse shows, and shopping for new equipment. It got me outside in the fresh air, connected me to nature, and gave me joy and a sense of accomplishment. This was a form of busyness, but it was also wonderful self-care.

In grief, find a balance to make time to feel it, but have awareness when you are in avoidance. There is nothing wrong with having a busy life. Not everyone has the luxury to maintain rigorous self-care routines. Self-care should not be another stressful thing to add to your long to-do list. However, for some people, tending to Conscious Grief will have to be scheduled.

This chapter explores how we maintain balance in times of distress. Self-care doesn't always have to equate to making an appointment for a massage or running a warm bath. I think it's about finding things that make you feel a sense of peace, things that relax you and calm your central nervous system.

In the midnineties, Margaret Stroebe and Henk Schut created the Dual Process Model for bereavement. Stroebe and Schut deduced that grief is best prescribed in doses. We need to feel the pain but also need to take a break from it and participate in normal activities of living (Williams 2014.)

The theory describes two different ways of behaving: Loss Orientated, which would be focusing on the person we have lost; for example, looking at photos, sharing memories, feeling the grief. The second is Restoration Orientated, which is distractions, moving on with life, and taking on new roles and identities. As we grieve, we move between both modes, going back and forth between loss and restoration. This is why it is called a dual process (Williams 2014).

My family stayed in the Restoration Orientated side and veered away from the Loss Orientated side. Moving between the two is wise; it is important to lean into the pain and feel it and then find the distractions that give you respite so grief does not consume you.

I interviewed Charlotte Maya, author of Sushi Tuesdays, who exemplifies the Dual Process Model of grieving. Charlotte's husband, Sam, took his own life and left her widowed at the age of thirty-nine with two young children, ages six and eight. Her husband had shown no previous signs of depression, and the shock and bewilderment left her with complicated grief.

In the weeks following Sam's death, Charlotte's weight dropped twenty-five pounds. Her friends worried as her clothes were noticeably hanging off her frail frame. Five months after Sam's death, Charlotte took herself for a run on the hiking trails in her home city of Pasadena. Out of sight and in nature, she put one foot in front of the other and began to run. She explained to me, "You can run out a lot of mad on the trails!" When she got back from that initial run, she felt hungry for the first time since Sam's death. Running became a therapy for her grief and gave her a sense of relief from being in her head all the time.

Charlotte wisely decided to designate one day a week to self-care. As a practical matter, the "day" lasted as long as the children's school schedule allowed, usually nine a.m. to two p.m. After dropping her children off at school, she would schedule the whole day around her nourishment. This would not include any social arrangements. The day's focus was solely on her. Every Tuesday, she attended a yoga class and made an appointment to speak with her therapist. Sometimes she would have a pedicure; some days she would stay in bed and cry.

On self-care Tuesday, she would occasionally treat herself to delicious food, and she found that sushi became a regular favorite! This commitment lasted for years, and it affectionately became known as her Sushi Tuesday.

I hope this catchy phrase may inspire you to make a day or evening in your week solely for your nourishment. Maybe it will be Self-Care Saturday or Ice Cream Sunday! It is a wonderful reminder to find the things that give us joy while we are suffering.

In this chapter, I am going to give you more ideas for how you can take care of yourself while you grieve.

THE WALLOW

I do love a good wallow!

I was not a sickly child, but I was suffering from low mood. Getting a day off from school from my mum was virtually impossible. I had to work really hard to persuade her I needed a wallow day! My favorite thing to do was make a bed on the sofa with my duvet and watch daytime television and movies.

Give yourself permission to do this now and again! It is healthy because some of us refuse to give ourselves the gift of doing nothing. We keep up the facade that everything is okay when, actually, we need to feel sorry for ourselves and let the tears flow and the grumbling commence.

How does the wallow look for you? It could be putting on a movie, eating ice cream out of the tub, drinking a bottle of wine, eating bags of crisps/chips. Turning the lights off, pulling the covers over your head, and isolating from the world. Again, I leave it open to personal interpretation.

Maybe you need to stay in bed, let the self-care go, get greasy hair, and be feral for a few days. Most importantly, do not judge yourself. Give yourself permission to relax, do nothing, be in the victim state, and just wallow! Life can be hard, and it is good to be reminded of the words and title of Megan Devine's book, Its Ok That You're Not OK! (Devine 2017).

I would advise putting a time limit on your wallow state, say an afternoon, a few days, a week; maybe you need months. You decide.

Essentially, a wallow is taking a rest. Are you giving yourself permission to rest and do nothing? Grief is exhausting. You will require rest.

If you find everyday has been like this, and days are leading to weeks and months and you are concerned, please consult your doctor about depression.

NUTRITION

An Ayurvedic Proverb says, "When diet is correct, medicine is of no need" (Carroll 2022).

Nourishing our body with healthy food—preferably organic, fresh whole foods—is important. We also need to make sure we are getting enough of the stress-reducing vitamins (B6, B12 and C) and enough minerals, especially iron and zinc.

Keep your body hydrated, especially if the tears are flowing regularly. Drink fruit teas, which taste good warm or cold. The ritual of making tea feels nourishing and comforting.

I craved sweetness: ice cream and chocolate. I think it was because I felt I had no sweetness left in my life. I struggled with food and bingeing for many years. Grief can affect our relationship with food.

I interviewed my sister, Polly Webb, nutritional therapist at Sound Eating, who reiterates the importance of regulating blood sugar. Often when we are in grief, we crave carbohydrates, sugars, and highly processed refined foods to seek the quick release of pleasure. While they are comforting, they can cause spikes in blood sugar levels when eaten in isolation. This, in turn, can lead to a rollercoaster of peaks and troughs, which cause more cravings for starchy and sugary foods.

Polly explains that by eating a balanced plate with protein, carbohydrates, and vegetables, you will achieve steady blood sugar levels, which will satiate you and reduce cravings. The protein and vegetables slow down the rate at which sugar is released into your bloodstream. Polly is a great believer in enjoying your food and suggests that "by all means, have your chocolate bar or pudding, but try and eat it after your main meal rather than on its own as a snack to help maintain steady blood sugar levels."

Increasing research is being carried out on our gut health, or microbiome, and the connection between the gut and the brain. Just how important fiber is in our diet in feeding these beneficial bacteria in our gut that play such a crucial role in our overall well-being is becoming more widely known. By increasing your intake of plant foods—fruit, vegetables, nuts, seeds, legumes, herbs, and spices—you will also be ingesting more polyphenols (plant chemicals), which your microbes use to fight disease. Our gut bacteria also produce hundreds of neurochemicals, that is, 95 percent of the body's supply of serotonin that the brain uses to regulate moods (Seal 2021).

If your appetite has been lost, try eating small regular meals or opting for smoothies with protein powder and added vitamins. Snacking on high fat plant foods such as avocado, nuts, and seeds is a great way to help get nutrients in. Try delicious nut butters on crackers or toast or add them to porridge.

A lot of shame can be associated with our behavior around food. If that is you, I feel you. I was in that place for years. I remember a lady in a workshop I participated in who admitted to eating a family size trifle as soon as she got into the car after buying it in the supermarket. She was so desperate to eat it but did not have a spoon, so she ate it with her credit card! We both laughed hysterically when she told me the story. I felt such relief at hearing someone else's compulsive eating habits.

This is why sharing in groups can be so helpful.

COMMUNITY

Are you the only person in your social circle who has been touched by a sad or traumatic event? Friends in your community are unsure how to react, and you are now finding them difficult to be around. Now is the time to find your "community."

I am an advocate of grief groups, self-development workshops, writing groups, and yoga retreats. When I look back through my life, I have always been attracted to groups. It started as Pony Club when I was nine years old. Later on, I found solace in the church by doing an Alpha Course at University. In my thirties, I attended Overeaters Anonymous meetings to try and get a handle on my behavior around food. Listening to others speak about their lives and challenges is enormously powerful. Having a learning orientation to life and being teachable builds resilience.

First, we realize we are not alone. Phew, big sigh of relief! Second, I truly believe that we are all teachers for one another. Sorry if I sound like a broken record. You will hear me say that over and over again! When we share the vulnerability of our hearts in a safe environment, I can guarantee that what you say will be helping someone else, which is a beautiful thing.

I explain at the start of the Conscious Grief Program that some weeks you will feel resistance and want to skip a session. I encourage people to break through this and show up and connect. Being authentic and sharing your struggle helps you, but it also helps someone else. A certain alchemy or healing magic happens in a group of people who are willing to be vulnerable with one another.

Research by psychologist Susan Pinker describes how storytelling synchronizes heartbeats. The research describes four small studies, each one with approximately twenty to thirty participants. In all four, subjects' heart rates were monitored via EKG while they listened to the same stories. The study found that subjects in the same group produced synchronized heart rate patterns that rose and fell at roughly the same times during the narrative (Pinker 2021).

So when we all listen to one another, we become connected physically through the heartbeat. We become one, which shows us that we are not alone. Essentially, we are part of one consciousness. I hope your grief will connect you to others.

Earlier, I mentioned being in a controlled environment, and I believe this is very important. The twelve-step recovery program does this well. The very name Anonymous at the end of each type of addiction gives the participant privacy. Everyone is adhering to the rule that what is shared in the room stays in the room. Our innermost vulnerabilities need to be held with reverence and respect.

We need to feel safe in order to share our grief, which is why it is important to find the right community for you.

MEDITATION

Sometimes it is not possible to share your experience with someone else. I interviewed healer and meditation teacher Emma Ball, who found this to be her experience when she was younger and grieving. She found a connection to her source through sitting in the quiet and going deep inside. Meditation builds a relationship with ourselves but also connects us to something greater.

I would advise starting small, just a few minutes each day. Sometimes I use meditation like prayer, and I ask for help and guidance. A typical by-product of being a bereaved child is over self-sufficiency. I have to remind myself I can ask for help from spirit or the universe.

At first, you might resist meditation and find it difficult. This is normal. Not all meditations are sitting still in silence. You can find guided meditations, walking meditations—and dancing is a form of meditation. You can do meditations with chanting. Try one of the mini meditations on my YouTube page, which are under ten minutes long and are great for beginners (Nash 2022).

WRITING

"I don't know what I think until I write it down," said Joan Didion (2020).

If sharing in a group and meditating does not resonate, you could consider putting pen to paper. Writing can be an extremely cathartic way to process emotions. Just as the quote above by Joan Didion suggests, you may well be surprised by what comes out. Writing can help us work things out, or work through things.

Put pen to paper, and remember, this is for you only. Be messy, make spelling mistakes, and stop worrying how it looks or sounds. Just give it a go!

Since I was seven years old, I have kept a diary. I had no idea back then that writing was an act of self-care. Throughout my teens, I would fill books and books with my dilemmas. My inner critic was loud; all the worry and self-loathing would come out on the page. While it is very depressing, boring, and repetitive to read, getting my feelings out on to the page helped me enormously.

A way of expressing anger or deep pain can be released through a technique called free form writing. You do not have to write full sentences, but you let rip with a pen and paper; sometimes for me, the paper has actually ripped where

I dug so deeply with my pen. Once I have released all the anger, resentment, and whatever else needs to come out, I destroy the piece of paper by burning it or tearing it to shreds, destroying that negativity and letting it go!

Writing letters to our loved ones and communicating the things that we did not get a chance to say, or say the things we wished we had said, is a healing thing to do. In Conscious Grief Series 1, I interviewed relationship expert Amanda Lambros, who says, "Grief is undelivered communication. It's the things we wish we could have said, would have said, the coulda, woulda, shoulda; some people didn't have the time to say the things they wanted to say."

Sometimes we have deep regrets on how little we showed up for our loved ones or how much time we spent in conflict with them. You can complete unfinished business with people after they have died. Write a letter and tell them the things you want to say. They will hear it and see it. It is not too late.

The act of writing is releasing these thoughts and worries onto the page. If I cannot sleep because something is on my mind, I reach for my journal and write the thoughts out. This helps move the trapped energy, and I find I can sleep afterwards.

The same can be done to ex partners or friends who have upset you, but I would advise against sending them the actual letter! Sometimes it is energetically enough to write our goodbyes and do a personal ceremony of letting go. More of this later in the Modern Mourning Chapter.

SETTING BOUNDARIES

"Boundaries are a part of self-care. They are healthy, normal, and necessary," said Doreen Virtue (LifeVersation 2018).

We may need to set boundaries around how much time we spend with others. Some people do not have the capacity to "hold space" for us. You need to decide if listening to the mundane complaints of others is something you find relaxing or stressful.

I will always remember a bereaved mother sharing a story about a friend of hers who had been complaining about her hairdresser. She wanted to shake her friend and say "Have you any idea how I wish the biggest challenge in my life right now was my highlights!" In grief, you may find your fuse is short and you are unable to listen to other people's trivial complaints.

Maintaining loving boundaries for yourself is important. You could have a text or email saved and copy and paste it as a reply, saying, "Sorry. I am not ignoring you, I just do not have the capacity to see many people right now. Thank you for your concern. Please do not forget about me. I so appreciate messages of support. I just do not have the energy for a full reply." If people are offended by this or cannot respect your wishes, let that be their problem.

Maybe you will need support on a practical level with things like grocery shopping or cooking. I had one lady in my grief group who had friends in event planning. These incredible friends put together a rota of people to check in with her. They even drew up to-do lists and stuck them around the house so no one was left to wonder *What can I do to help?*

HOW TO HELP ME LIST
Many people will say "Let me know if there is anything you need." Have a list ready of things that you want help with. Quite likely, you are dealing with one of the hardest things that has ever happened in your life.

BE BOLD AND ASK:
1. Can you pick up xyz from the grocery store?
2. Can you message these people and tell them about the funeral?
3. Can you take over for a couple of hours? I need to be alone and rest.
4. I need help with picking my kids up from school.
5. I have not managed to walk my dog/clean out the hamster cage/take my pet to the vet. Can you help me please?
6. I am having a hard time with paying and organizing bills that my partner used to handle. Can you help with that?
7. I could use help moving some furniture around.
8. Organizing the will and probate is scaring me. Can you advise me on this?
9. Can you sit with me while I go through their things?
10. I would like company while watching a movie or TV show.
11. Can you help me address thank-you cards for the flowers I received?
12. I have no idea how to work this technology. Can you help me with this?

Sadly, you will find some people will not step up in the way you had imagined. Some friendships change and fall away. This is par for the course and one of the secondary losses that can be hurtful. More on this later in the book.

LOVING KINDNESS/COMPASSION

As you companion yourself in grief, be compassionate with yourself. You are going through something incredibly hard. You don't have to "buck up" and get on with it.

If being kind and loving to yourself feels foreign or hard to do, imagine yourself as the five-year-old you and connect with that little you inside. How would you talk to yourself? I hope you would be kind and gentle. You would wrap your arms around the little you and give yourself a big, warm hug. You would let the little you sob into your chest and let the little one rest.

Please, practice that with yourself right now. You won't win prizes for getting through grief as fast as possible. The vast majority of us are living overstressed and busy lives. If you are at work, take a minute to ground your feet under the desk and take a few gentle breaths or seek sunlight from a window and bathe in it for thirty seconds. Offer yourself a positive affirmation like "I am loved and supported" and bring yourself into the present moment for thirty seconds.

Even better, if you can take one hour a week to tend to your heart—in a sound healing, a meditation, a yoga class, engagement with nature—please give yourself that gift. It might mean waking up one hour earlier to be alone if you have a family or full days.

ANIMALS

After my stepfather left, my mother accidentally ran over his black Labrador called Becky. Becky stayed living with us because I was so fond of her. She was very elderly. I was devastated, and so was my mother! Months later, my mother reluctantly agreed to getting the most adorable Jack Russel puppy we called Percy. Despite her initial resistance to another dog to take care of, little Percy became the absolute love of her life. He brought so much joy and laughter into our lives when we really needed it. Percy became the man of the house and quite the guard dog!

Scientific research has proven that spending time with animals can lower the stress hormone cortisol, making them wonderful stress relievers (Science Daily 2019).

In Conscious Grief Series 1, I interviewed Clare Milford Haven, founder of James' Place. Clare's eldest son, James, died by suicide at the age of twenty-one. In response to his tragic and untimely death, Clare set up this charity to give men who are in suicidal crisis a safe haven to seek support. When I asked Clare where she found solace from her grief, she said, "Animals." An avid rider and dog lover, she remarked, "I have embraced nature and animals a lot more. Animals are uncomplicated; people are complicated. Animals give you unconditional love and are very comforting; they don't ask you too many questions!"

I wholeheartedly agree. Animals are wonderful companions. Their presence keeps us connected to our hearts and gives us purpose to take care of them when we feel hopeless.

NATURE

Choosing to get a pet may not be an option for you. But getting a house plant or growing some herbs or vegetables in your garden might be possible. I have a small fig tree in my tiny flat. It only needs watering once a week, but I take great delight in remembering to care for my tree and seeing new leaves grow. My green fingers have not found their way to a vegetable patch for now.

My sister, Lisa, has a greenhouse with cucumbers and tomatoes growing in it. Witnessing how a small seed can grow to an edible vegetable allows our minds to be awed by nature. When we are grieving, our thoughts can be black; nature helps us to lift the veil and see new life and hope.

Scientific researcher Dr. Chris Lowry from Bristol University found that touching soil has an antidepressant effect. It releases serotonin in the brain. Tending to plants and getting your hands covered in soil will not only make you feel better, but it has also been linked to improving your immune system as well (Science Daily 2007).

Being near water, around trees, or in the mountains brings the same feeling. We are on this planet, which is full of diversity, awesomeness, and wonder. Keep your eyes open to the beauty that surrounds us.

BEAUTY

Beauty lifts our vibration, making us feel good. The environment we live in is important. While you grieve, make your environment comfortable and pleasing to be in. Light scented candles, buy fresh flowers, and burn incense. Make your space sacred while you go through this passage of grieving.

Grief will deplete you; find what nourishes you.

Self-care can come in many forms. It could be the Epsom salt bath, creative outlets, setting boundaries, saying no, saying yes, slowing down, lying down, watching films all day, walking in nature, caring for animals, or attending to plants. Find what works for you.

HEART WORK

- Take five deep breaths, in through your nose, filling your belly, and gently exhale through your mouth.

- What, if any, are your concerns with wallowing, and how will you try to overcome this?

- What does your wallow or taking rest look like?

- Make a commitment to yourself to take a walk, swim, journal, shake or dance; maybe it's once a week, maybe it's daily—you decide.

- Eat something delicious and savor every bite.

- Ask for help; delegate where you can.

- Take a blanket, lie down outside, and watch the clouds.

- Make a playlist that makes your heart sing.

- Stay hydrated.

- What boundaries do you need to set to prioritize your needs?

- Elevate the vibration of your home with scent, flowers, or something beautiful.

- Buy a journal and start writing about your feelings, hopes, and desires.

Put this list on your fridge door!

CHAPTER 3

Beliefs

Rumi said, "Don't be satisfied with stories, how things have gone with others. Unfold your own myth" (Barks and Moyne 2004, 41.)

Death is always a shock and a mystery. In times of great pain or grief, we may reach out to God or some higher power to help us, or we may find that our beliefs have shifted and changed in the wake of a tragic circumstance. No one can be 100 percent sure what happens when we die, but it leads us to ponder some of life's big questions.

My sisters and I were raised going to Sunday school in the Christian Science church. We were armchair Christian Scientists and attended sporadically. My paternal grandparents were part of this community, and we went because they did. At bedtime, we read Bible stories, and I would pray if I could not sleep at night or was afraid of the dark. At school, we said grace before meals and recited the Lord's Prayer in morning assembly. I had Christian teachings throughout my British education.

After my father died, a spiritual void coincided with the presence of my stepfather. Once he had left, my mother reinitiated her relationship with Jesus and became a born-again Christian. I was in my early teens, and my mum was encouraging me in this direction. I had been seeking since my dad died, asking questions like what is the point of life? Where do we go when we die? His death made me a seeker. This Christian narrative promised to have all the answers to my existence, so I was intrigued.

My mother found refuge and peace in the teachings of Jesus. I found myself obsessing about the concept of heaven and hell and for the most part did not find it peaceful at all. They offered a lot of rules—like no sex before marriage—and I was not sure if I agreed with them or not. By then, I had very little trust and safety in my place in the world. I started to internalize the belief that if I was good, Jesus would protect me and bad things would stop happening. I was almost forcing myself to believe these things and honestly getting more fearful than anything else.

My wonderful godparents, Roger and Ros Kite, told my mother a story when I was fifteen that pricked my ears and raised my curiosity about the afterlife. Rewind to the midnineties. Stephanie, their daughter, was very ill with post viral fatigue syndrome and feeling lost in her life. One of Stephanie's friends talked about a medium called Mrs. Worzel who lived nearby. Out of the blue, Stephanie announced to her friend, "I need to go and see Mrs. Worzel!" So she walked down the road, knocked on her door, and was welcomed in.

Mrs. Worzel asked, "Can you give me a piece of jewelry to hold?" The reading started like this, and the medium relayed accurate and personal details about a recent situation in Stephanie's life.

After this, she said, "Oh, hang on a minute. I've got a gentleman here." She started laughing and went on. "He wants me to say, 'Can you stop wearing so much bloody black!'" She continued. "He's blond, and he's happy he's got a dog with him who's really, really blond. He's blond, his dog's blond. He is doing great and helping his wife, who is still here, make the right decisions."

Stephanie knew that was my dad, Peter. He was with our Golden Retriever, named Blondie, who had also recently died. Just for the record, my dad and Stephanie's dad were cousins and close friends, which is why Roger became my godfather.

I thought this was fascinating! Interestingly, my mother relayed the story to me but dismissed it and said we must not believe in things like that because of the church teaching we followed. I was amazed. What a fun message to receive. Our dad was with our dog Blondie, and he was still present in some form! I was curious but afraid in equal measure because of the church teachings.

This could have been a beautiful opportunity for my mum and me to have had a reading and for us to have processed our grief together. We could have shared my dad's presence and guidance in our lives. Instead, it was dismissed that, in doing such a thing, we were dancing with the devil. It would take me another twenty years to connect with my father through a medium.

As part of my research for my death and grieving thesis while studying spiritual psychology, I finally plucked up the courage to find a medium and book a reading.

My reading was a profound experience. The medium immediately gave evidence that she was connected to my parents. The words she gave me were so precise, things she could never have known. I wished I had recorded it, but I wrote things down. It made me realize that my parents were watching over me and guiding me. I can still ask them for help and communicate with them. It is possible to have a relationship with them, even though they are not here in the physical realm.

Since that first reading, I have had several more over the years. Occasionally, I crave that intimate connection with my parents, just to remind myself that they are with me. I limit my readings because I think it is important we act with agency and learn to trust our own intuition.

In grief, it is common for our beliefs to shift and change. As much as I found myself distancing from church, I know other people are drawn to it in times of crisis. Whichever way it is does not matter. Find what gives you a sense of peace and strength.

It is interesting to notice how big life transitions can open us up to new possibilities.

MODELING JESUS

Grief specialist Gary Roe educates licensed therapists on grief. Gary chose this path because his childhood was mired in grief and trauma. He had been sexually abused by multiple predators. Then, at the age of twelve, a boy in his class died suddenly of spinal meningitis, and little Gary was asking the big questions like "Why did this happen? I don't get this. I don't like this!"

His home life was chaotic. His mother and father had a volatile relationship that ended in divorce. Shortly after the separation, his mother suffered from a mental breakdown, at which point he went to live with his father, who one day collapsed in front of him and was rushed to the hospital when Gary was just fifteen years old.

In the hospital, Gary spent seven days sitting with his father, who was in a critical condition. This gave him time to memorize his face, say everything he wanted to say, ask for forgiveness, and say his goodbyes. It seems like no coincidence that he had this sacred number of seven days where Gary had some big awakenings for a young boy. He said to himself, I need to prepare myself; I need to figure out how to heal and grow and use this for good. If I can't do that, then what is this all about?

Gary studied psychology, and after school, he became a pastor and missionary and has lived in different countries around the world. He has written over ten books that have helped countless people, and he found his purpose in Jesus. Gary's essence and way of being reflects the teachings of

Jesus. I found Gary to be a very compassionate and beautiful man to sit with and interview.

He talks of his work as "walking alongside hurting and grieving people as they hurt and grieve and just reminding them of the things that are common in grief and that this is not forever. Remind them they are not alone, even though they feel alone. Tell them, you are not crazy even though you feel crazy. You will get through this, and if you are willing to learn what loss can teach you, there is no end for the good you can do."

JEWISH RITUALS

On the other end of the spectrum, you might be an atheist like author Colin Campbell. Colin Cambell is an atheist, but his wife Gail is Jewish. They decided to raise their children as Jews and they joined a Temple. Tragically, they were driving from Los Angeles to Joshua Tree when a drunk driver crashed into their car. Their teenage children, Ruby and Hart, were in the back seat and were both killed. Colin and Gail survived. In the aftermath of complete turmoil, Colin found the Jewish rituals and traditions to be like an anchor for their grieving process (Campbell 2023).

In Judaism, it is important for community to witness their grief. After the funeral, Jewish mourners open their home for others to come and sit Shiva with them for seven days. This ritual follows rules like not looking in the mirror, wearing the same shirt, and not shaving or cutting hair. The reason for this is because mourners feel broken on the inside, so they want their outward appearance to reflect this. Sitting Shiva then becomes Shloshim, which lasts for thirty days after the funeral. Colin and Gail found that these rituals gave them direction and purpose, and it included others. Their grief was not a process they did alone.

Colin wrote Finding the Words: Working Through Profound Loss with Hope and Purpose, which offers an alternative path for processing pain that is active, vocal, and truly honors loved ones lost (Campbell 2023).

After reading Colin's book, I reflected on when my father died. We were casual Sunday school attendees, not rooted in the community. We did not have a priest or spiritual elder come to guide us or impart wisdom. I think that would have given a communal sense to our process, which we never had. From that day, my grief became individualized and difficult to talk about.

Many religions have rituals that bring comfort and closure surrounding death. Essentially all religions are pointed toward love and connection. Grief makes us feel disconnected, isolated, and fragmented, so anything that brings us toward love and connection helps us feel whole again.

FROM ATHEISM TO SPIRITUALITY

Sophie Mills discovered my work and subscribed to my newsletter. When I asked if people were willing to share their grief stories of spiritual transformation, Sophie replied. We found a time to meet on Zoom between our time zones, Australia and England. I was fascinated to hear her story.

Sophie was raised in an atheist household where death, sex, and emotions were considered taboo topics. She was praised for her stoic strength and believed that we only have one shot at life and, therefore, everything had to be perfect.

When her beloved father died, her world was turned upside down, and the tsunami tidal wave of grief hit her hard. Sophie realized she was surrounded by people similar to herself—people who were unable to express their emotions—and she felt very alone and isolated in her pain.

A chiropractor was the catalyst for her spiritual seeking. He suggested books on grief for Sophie to read, and that was when she began giving herself permission to feel. Her scientific background as an occupational therapist made her look for scientific, research-based literature. She found appreciation for Dr. Joe Dispenza and Bruce Lipton, who are masters at joining the scientific and spiritual worlds.

Sophie did a lot of somatic healing: crying, journaling, screaming into pillows, and trance dancing to help her move the energy of her grief. Sophie became particularly intrigued by how the body holds pain and trained to become a Body Talk Practitioner. Sophie has done many women's circles and believes wholeheartedly in the power of sharing and having your grief witnessed.

The death of her father changed Sophie's perspective and beliefs on her existence. Now she believes that we have many lives, that our consciousness lives on, and that life is happening for us, not against us.

Her prolific reading about grief and understanding her emotional landscape laid the foundation and tools to deal with the heartbreaking death of her newborn baby. She said this new awareness and seeing life from the spiritual perspective gave her the tools to cope with the grief of losing a child. Sophie is on a mission to have a Grief Revolution because she has the experience of awakening due to the death of her father. She sees grief as a powerful catalyst of shifting her whole perspective on life.

FINDING PURPOSE

I discovered Uma Girish while researching the term Conscious Grief. I reached out to her to see if she would like to participate in Conscious Grief Series 2, and she graciously accepted. Uma was born in India and spent her younger years aspiring to the ideas of Western culture, of independence and freedom. She wanted to break away from the Eastern way of doing things and enjoy her own autonomy of being.

When her dear Amma (mother) died of breast cancer, Uma had recently moved to Chicago, where she was devoid of family and friends and far from her home culture. She returned to India to say her final goodbye to her mother. While wrapping her mother's body in a silk sari, the awareness dropped in that we are born with nothing and we die with nothing.

This made Uma ponder everything. Why were we so conditioned to keep acquiring things when ultimately we get to take nothing. This is when her transformation journey and asking the questions began. Who am I? Why am I here? What is the purpose of my life? How am I meant to serve? What really matters in my life?

Uma was in her midforties, and she started to recalibrate with the teachings of her Hindu culture that she had dismissed earlier in her life.

When she returned to Chicago, she found a church that offered a nine-week course for people who were grieving. Being in a community of grievers was an important part of her process, and she recognized that India's strength is community, which she missed in the US.

The big questions that she found herself pondering led her to work with a spiritual mentor. With the guidance of this teacher, Uma processed difficult emotions like the guilt for not being with her mother when she died.

Uma explained that she allowed herself to cry a lot. Crying was modeled to her by her mother, so this came easily and naturally. She allowed time and space for these healing tears. At one stage, her husband asked, "When are you going to stop crying so much?" Uma replied that she did not know when she would stop crying.

Somewhere in her heart, Uma knew that she wanted to use her pain to serve other people. She trained to become a hospice volunteer and sat with the dying for over five years. She said she could be in that place of pain and hold space for others. Uma cautions against volunteering to escape what people need to feel but encourages sitting with difficult emotions.

This is an important point. We don't want to bypass our own pain in our service. It is important for us to feel it and move through it.

Uma is now a published author of three books, a spiritual teacher and mentor, and supports others in grief and transformation. Her Amma is her angel and guide. She speaks to her often and receives signs from her in the shape of hearts. The funny thing about the day I interviewed her, I chose to wear a knitted sweater with hearts on!

SIGNS

When people die, we can find extraordinary signs and messages from the other side. Bizarre synchronicities may occur. This might be the first time you have ever noticed this kind of thing. Some people will dismiss this as woo-woo or challenge you about believing in such things.

It is up to us to decide if things are coincidences or spiritual guidance. If these signs are a comfort to you, embrace them and don't share them with people who dismiss it. Another good reason to find a grief community.

You might see feathers, little birds, coins, messages on car license plates, flickering lights, the television coming on by itself, or their favorite song playing on the radio at the perfect moment. I do believe their spirit is communicating with us, and we just don't always see it or believe it.

I know some people do not advocate readings with mediums because of the concern that people can become reliant on this connection and unable to move forward in the physical world reality. Sadly, charlatans will take advantage of people spending their money in this way. My advice is: choose to have your reading with someone who calls themselves an "Evidential Medium." This means they will give you hard evidence that they have connected with your loved ones. They will do this with specific names or details. Another indication of a medium with integrity is that they will limit how many times they will read for you. They will not continue to see you on a regular basis as they know this is not healthy.

EVIDENTIAL MEDIUM SUZANNE GIESEMANN

I had the honor of interviewing medium Suzanne Giesemann in Conscious Grief Series 1. I found Suzanne particularly interesting because for the first four and a half decades of her life, she did not connect to spirits. In her former career, she was a navy commander and commanding officer who served as an aide to the chairman of the Joint Chiefs of Staff on 9/11. After the 9/11 attack, Suzanne decided life was short, so she retired and pursued a lifelong dream of sailing around the world. With perspective, she now describes this as an attempt to run from the atrocity of grief that 9/11 left in its wake.

While Suzanne and her husband were sailing around the world, they got the news that her pregnant stepdaughter had been struck by lightning and killed. They suffered the double loss of their soon-to-be grandchild and their daughter. It was this devastating circumstance that left Suzanne seeking answers about the afterlife.

This led her on a new path and career as she realized she could connect with her stepdaughter's spirit and the spirits of others' loved ones. She went to study at the world-renowned Arthur Findlay College for psychic studies in Stansted, England.

Suzanne is slim, with short, thick hair, conventional, and smart looking. The way she speaks is articulate and to the point. I found this refreshing, a sort of no-nonsense educator type tone. Having a reading with a good medium can be a huge source of comfort for someone struggling with grief. Suzanne says, "Life is eternal, and love never dies." It gives the griever hope that they will see their loved ones again and that it is possible to establish a new relationship with them in spirit. This offers hope and reassurance that we are never alone.

Suzanne gives an energetic explanation of grief and describes us all as "energy beings," and says that we create energy fields with others. When that has gone, we feel incomplete and our sense of wholeness changes. Suzanne informs us that "what happens with grief is, we have someone we love, and we create a field with them, a pattern of energy that creates a wholeness with us. So, with death or divorce, part of that field is gone, and you feel incomplete. Which is why you feel like there is a hole in your heart. The pattern of your very being has changed. So, grief lasts until you adjust to that change and create new patterns of being."

The work of a medium is to help people understand that life continues across the veil/after we die, and we can form a new pattern of being with the ones we love who are no longer in their physical body. Meditation is one way to connect with our loved ones on the other side, and Suzanne teaches courses on how to make a connection with a spirit.

If she had not experienced the profound pain and loss of her pregnant stepdaughter, this journey of seeking may not have happened. Ultimately, we are all seeking a sense of wholeness, and our awakening begins when we realize there is a greater sense of reality and we are all connected.

Suzanne shares, "As you go through this journey, you will find that the pain is so bad that you seek answers, and that we are souls, that we are so much more than our bodies. We seek new ways of being and a greater compassion to others who are suffering."

Wise words indeed.

BELIEFS ABOUT YOURSELF

During grief, we might be holding strong judgments against ourselves. We will explore guilt in greater detail in Chapter Five, Feel the Feelings. However, I want to include a little bit here right now about the story you might be creating about what has happened in your life.

For example, you hear the phrase "Good things happen to good people." I used to think maybe we were bad people and that was why bad things happened to us. I remember hearing teachings at church about having Eastern artifacts or art in your home could be welcoming negative spirits into your life. I was scouring our home for things that might be bringing dark energy that I needed to clear. I was afraid and somehow making myself responsible for what was happening.

In my practice as a grief guide, I hear a lot of self-blame for why someone has died or a relationship has ended. The negative voice in our heads, sometimes referred to as the inner critic, can be incredibly destructive. This requires attention, and I would advise working with a therapist or coach to start rewiring your thoughts. What we think and say to ourselves impacts us physically, mentally, emotionally, and spiritually.

The fascinating work of Japanese scientist Dr. Masaru Emoto found that the molecular structure of water was affected by human words, intentions, and vibrations. In his book The Hidden Messages in Water, Emoto demonstrates in his experiment that when the water is given words of adoration and praise, beautiful frozen flakes are created. However, if the water is given a negative frequency of criticism and fearful thoughts and words, then the snowflakes are disfigured and unpleasant looking (Emoto 2005, xxiv).

Our bodies are primarily made up of water, so imagine what damage we might be imparting on ourselves with negative and harmful thoughts. How we think affects everything. While grieving, we get confusing and conflicting messages from people around us, which we will explore in more depth in the next chapter.

Observe the beliefs and the thoughts you are internalizing. They might sound crazy and irrational to say out loud. Make a note of them in your journal. I share tools in chapter six on ways to work with negative beliefs.

YOU DECIDE

Belief systems help us bear the unbearable. This might be the first time you have given any thought to the afterlife or the significance of religion and belief systems. Your conscious grieving may open up new thought processes and deeper conversations about life and your existence.

I often think of life as a theme park. Sometimes we are on the merry-go-round or the Ferris wheel, and sometimes it's the wild roller coaster that scares the life out of us. Every ride has something to teach us or a way to expand ourselves.

HEART WORK

- Are you angry with God/the universe?

- What beliefs were you raised with? Have your beliefs changed?

- What are some of the rituals of the culture you were raised in that have helped you in grief?

- What beliefs do you have about what has happened?

- Do you have an inner critic? How loud is that voice right now?

EXPRESSION

CHAPTER 4

Triggers

What is a trigger?

"In psychology, a trigger' is a stimulus that causes a painful memory to resurface. A trigger can be any sensory reminder of the traumatic event: a sound, sight, smell, physical sensation, or even a time of day or season" (Pedersen 2022).

We are going to stumble into trigger zones in our grief. Grief is painful, and we are in a highly sensitive state. Many of the people around us will not be able to understand or relate. To grieve consciously, we will become aware of our triggers and our responses.

You might be walking around looking at other people happily going about their days, and internally, you are screaming, Why is everyone so bloody happy! My world has imploded; no one understands.

Feeling triggered provides good information that you have hurt inside that needs to be voiced.

In this chapter, we will look at some common ways our grief can be triggered. These can be obvious and, other times, we can merrily be moving forward with our lives, thinking grief is in the rearview mirror. Then something happens and whoosh, we are blindsided by crushing grief again. Do not be dismayed; as much as this can feel frustrating and like you are failing somehow, you are not. Deep love that has been lost will always be felt and remembered.

MY MOTHER DIED, AND MY TRIGGERS BEGAN

My mother remained at home in bed the last six months of her life. The breast cancer moved to her liver, and her condition declined. My eldest sister, Lisa, moved back into our family home and took care of her. My middle sister, Polly, would come on weekends to help. I was at university, and they decided, because I am the youngest, they would protect me and let me get on with my studies.

During the end of my mother's life, she had a strong faith in Christianity. Many people were praying for her cancer to be healed. I was in denial, thinking the cancer would surely go and a miracle would happen. I could not imagine that God would be that cruel and leave me without any parents. However, I witnessed that my mum was tired of life. She had had so much cumulative grief in a short number of years. Her faith allowed her to surrender to death. She was longing to be reunited with my father in spirit.

I had the phone call from Lisa saying, "You need to come home. Mummy is not doing well."

The following day, I returned home. I remember hearing my mother's breath loudly rattle. I ran up the spiral staircase and went into her room. The loud breathing stopped, and I held her hand. Then I realized she had died. I felt calm. This always amazes me. I called for Lisa and the nurse, who happened to be in the house at the time. They came upstairs, and the nurse confirmed she had died. Our dear mum, Penny, experienced a peaceful transition and was ready to die. She did not fight it. She was at home, in her beautiful bed. It was a good death.

Family and friends came to her bedside to say their last goodbye to her lifeless body. It was a hot summer's day, June 4, 2002. My memories are blurred. In these moments, finding appropriate words is hard. What I do remember is the sentence shared with me: "She is in a better place now." It was the last thing I wanted to hear. My mother—my only parent—had just left me, and I was barely an adult. I needed her. I did not want her to be in heaven or in a better place; I wanted her to be here with me. I wanted to be like everyone else around me with a parent, or two.

With years of perspective, I know those words came from a well-meaning and loving place.

Some people will read that and vehemently disagree with me and argue that saying "She is in a better place now" is always a bad idea. That is the thing with grief: some comments may activate you, but for others, those comments will be comforting. Grievers are a tricky bunch!

My mother died aged fifty-seven, and it was too soon. She was not going to be there to see me get married, have a baby, advise me on business, send me recipes, take shopping trips with me, travel, or be a grandmother! Our mother could have had another thirty or forty more years with us, but it was not to be. I think my sisters and I knew on a deeper level that she was ready to leave, and we respected that, however hard it was. I admire her courage for not being afraid to embrace the next adventure, which was death.

The story of my mother's peaceful accepting death might be a trigger for you. I am sorry if it is.

STICKS AND STONES

Do you remember that saying "Sticks and stones will break my bones, but words will never hurt me?" I often think of this outdated mantra and how untrue it is. Words do matter and can trigger us more than anything, especially in grief.

Some people tell me they cannot connect to anger. However, when asked to think of unhelpful comments people have said, that usually activates some anger! I teach people that this is a healthy emotion to feel and process.

We do not want to repress or deny anger, because this is when it becomes physically and emotionally toxic. More on this in later chapters.

When I interviewed fertility expert and acupuncturist Emma Cannon, she joked about the "muggles," people who are not

touched by grief and pain. These people will often offer us
unhelpful platitudes in response to our loss.

IRRITATING COMMENTS

At least… you have another child.
Everything happens for a reason.
It's only a dog/cat/etc.
You have to be strong for…
Time is a healer.
They are in a better place now.
Keep busy.
He/she wanted to be with… in heaven.
You are so brave.
You are so strong.
I know just how you feel.
This is God's plan.
In which grief stage are you in?
You are young; you can marry again.
You can have more children.
Are you over it yet?
Count your blessings.
Don't cry.
Don't cry in front of…
They would want you to be happy.
Everything will be okay.

IRRITATING COMMENTS FOLLOWING
A RELATIONSHIP BREAKUP

There are plenty more fish in the sea.
You are better off without them.

I never liked them anyway.
You can do better.

A WISE MAN ONCE SAID NOTHING

Sometimes the best thing to do with a grieving friend is to be present and listen. It's hard because silence makes a lot of people feel uncomfortable. When we are grieving, we need to be shown that people love us and want to be there for us. We do not need to be fixed.

Ultimately, we have all said the wrong thing to someone who was grieving. Grieving people are highly sensitive, and due to the unique nature of grief, it is easy to get it wrong.

If you are battling with yourself for saying the wrong thing in the past, let it go! No one is perfect.

I like to think people are trying their best. If you have the energy, it could be an opportunity to educate someone and tell them that their words are not helpful. Even people who have been through traumatic events may not be the most compassionate. Grief does not come with a one-size-fits-all label.

HELPFUL THINGS TO HEAR

You don't have to talk; I will just sit with you.
I am so, so sorry.
I am here to listen.
I love you, and I am here for you.
Would you like a hug?

Would you like to talk?

Tell me about... their personality/their life.

I don't know how you feel, but I am here to help however I can.

When you are ready, tell me what you need.

I loved them so very much.

I will always remember them for...

SPECIAL DAYS

Holidays, birthdays, and anniversaries used to be happy days of celebration, but they are now difficult. Weddings were a trigger for me. They reminded me of what I did not have. I never aspired to have a big, white wedding because who would walk me down the aisle or take me wedding dress shopping? I would either drink too much or feel miserable while everyone else was having a great time. Remember, for a long time, I was pushing my grief down instead of integrating it into my life as I do now.

When I interviewed Elizabeth Boisson from the incredible Helping Parents Heal organization, it was approaching Thanksgiving and Christmas. The interview date landed on her son Morgan's thirty-third birthday, which was a wonderful way to honor him. Two of Elizabeth's children have transitioned; her daughter Chelsea, when she was two days old in 1991, and Morgan in 2009 from severe altitude sickness while on a student trip to the Base Camp of Mount Everest in Tibet. When Morgan passed, she felt him hug her. From that day, she wanted to connect with other parents who had lost a child but felt their spiritual presence. This experience was the beginning of Helping Parents Heal.

Elizabeth says how children in spirit love to be remembered. Some parents in their community leave a seat at the table on holiday celebrations, placing a photo of them at their seat. While this might be a hard thing to do in fear of triggering other people, because they might find it weird, she encourages parents to do what feels right for them.

Every year, Elizabeth creates a holiday card with a photo of her family on the front. Inside the card, she places a photo of the family with Morgan from when he was younger, and on the back of the card, she puts a solo photo of Morgan. Elizabeth says, "I want people to understand that he is an integral part of our family and always will be. I think it's becoming more and more acceptable for people to keep talking about their loved ones who have transitioned in spirit despite the fact they might have transitioned twelve years ago, or thirty years ago for Chelsea. To keep having them as part of our conversation."

Holidays, anniversaries, and birthdays are not going to be the same. Our hearts will long for those we miss. However, we can choose to integrate our loved ones into celebrations as Elizabeth demonstrates to soften those triggers.

THE ORDINARY AND MUNDANE MOMENTS

While the holidays and anniversaries can pierce our hearts, so, too, can the ordinary moments. Food is central to our lives, and this simple and pleasurable ritual can be a reminder of the people we miss. One lady in my grief group shared that pineapple was her husband's favorite fruit.

Now she walks past the pineapples at the store and her heart drops. This an example of the mundane moments that trigger our grief.

Seasons and the weather can bring us back to the moment someone passed or was unwell.

The sounds of ambulance sirens and lights remind you of a fateful night or day.

You might see someone in a crowd or on a bus who looks just like your loved one. Suddenly, your body is filled with sadness at the reminder they are no longer here.

I interviewed poet Chanel Brenner in Conscious Grief Series 2. One of her most popular poems is titled "Fucking RiteAid." Chanel's grief for her young son, Riley, was triggered when she saw a toy he would have loved in this popular Californian store. Chanel worked with a hypnotherapist to help soften the pain and continue shopping there (Brenner 2014).

One of the editors who helped me with this book shared how she always went bra shopping with her mother. Now she has a hard time shopping for underwear because it reminds her of her mother.

Our clever smart phones create memories and movies, bringing the past right into our palms. At times, this can be too painful. Remember the idea of dosing your grief. Once upon a time, we had to reach for an album to see photos; now, through social media and our phone photo library, they can be accessed in an instant and sometimes involuntarily. It is possible to turn this function off on your phone. Ask Google to show you what to do.

Way back before smart phones, I remember not wanting to delete my mother's contact number. It felt too sad and final. How could I not have my mum in my phone anymore? Eventually, I lost the phone and all the contacts, which took care of that for me.

The once simple task of filling out a form now becomes loaded with emotion. Your emergency contact person is no longer here. You have to tick the widow or widower box, and this leaves you feeling vulnerable and alone.

You might experience vivid dreams about loved ones who have passed. I know I have woken in floods of tears on many occasions after having dreams about my mother.

Major life transitions or achievements like graduations and having children can stir up feelings of grief as you wish the person you lost could be there to witness and participate in these life changes.

I have experienced many instances when I have longed for the guidance of my parents and wished they were here to offer their insights and wisdom.

A song is played on the radio and transports you back in time to a treasured moment with your loved one.

GRIEFBURSTS

When I first read about griefbursts, it was a huge aha moment for me. I was reading Understanding Your Grief: Ten Essential Touchstones for Finding Hope and Healing Your Heart by Dr. Alan D. Wolfelt. He writes, "You may feel an overwhelming sense of missing the person you loved and find yourself openly crying or perhaps even sobbing." He says that these moments can come completely without warning. Sometimes people phrase them as grief attacks, and they can also be triggered by things like food, photos, music, or a movie (Wolfelt 2023, 75.)

After my mum died, I started to have griefbursts. I was unable to trace them back to grief. Since it was a year or more after she died, I thought it must be something else in my life. I had no awareness of how we process grief or trauma. I do not remember experiencing any specific trigger, but I would start crying and be unable to stop.

When I look back, I wish I had more knowledge about grief and how it creeps up on us and that we can only repress it for so long. My body needed a release through these enormous outpouring of tears. It felt out of control and confusing, and sadly, I blamed the relationship I was in for my unhappiness.

The pain of losing both my parents, my anchors in this world, needed to be acknowledged. Those healing tears were releasing toxins. It is amazing how intelligent our bodies are. It took me years to understand!

If you find yourself crying uncontrollably, know that this is grief. When this happens, excuse yourself from work if you have to. Take the day off and let the tears fall.

FRIENDSHIPS

Some friends and family will want you to move on quickly. They will not like the grieving you. They may want to try and be cheerful and jolly around you and tell you to keep busy. They will think sitting in negative emotions is a bad thing, but this is because pain makes them uncomfortable.

Some friends will immediately want to relate by telling you how they felt when they went through something. This might feel frustrating, draining, and annoying. In grief, comparing yourself is not helpful. Our grief is unique and personal to us.

A difficult part of grief is accepting that some friends are not equipped to handle tragedy and pain. You will feel let down. They don't know what to say, so they disappear. It is hard to assimilate why some people are unable to be there for grieving friends, but unfortunately, it is part of the shit parcel. I think most people are unable to find the right words. So people fret; they worry they will say the wrong thing and then they say nothing at all.

Finding the Words: Working Through Profound Loss with Hope and Purpose is a brilliant book by Colin Campbell that I referenced in Chapter 3. Colin and his wife Gail's car was hit by a drunk driver, and their teenage children sitting in the back seat were killed. Colin found so many people wrote "There are no words" as a message of condolence. I hold my hands up. I too have been partial to this sentence, particularly in the face of such tragic circumstances. These words never felt helpful for Colin because it stopped the conversation as if there was nothing to say. He needed to talk about his grief and his dear children, Ruby and Hart (Campbell 2023, 6).

I was impressed by Colin and Gail as they became adept at asking people for what they needed. Grief is so unique, and some phrases will be of comfort to some, and the same phrase could send the next person into deep rage. Therefore, Colin advises the reader to create a "Grief Spiel" that lays out how you would like to be treated, which platitudes you cannot abide, and invite friends to share stories about the people you love and have lost. Colin found that people offered help, but he needed to find tasks that they could help with. By doing this, he included people in his grief journey and strengthened bonds within his community (Campbell 2023, 54).

It takes energy to direct people in this way, but I think it is brilliant if you have the tenacity to do so. It may end up that friends who might have drifted away, out of fear, will instead be there for you because you've taught them how to better support you in your grief.

JEALOUSY

This is a tough one. It is no one else's fault that their family or relationship is healthy, alive, and intact. However, the reality is, we may envy other people who have what we no longer have. This can make us want to distance from them because their happy families trigger our grief.

Someone in my grief group described rage building up in her as she watched a multigenerational family at the table next to her. They had their mum and dad; their children had their grandparents. In that moment, she felt the surge of jealousy rush through her.

Know that this is natural. That lady admitted to those feelings in the safe space of our Conscious Grief Program. Airing the feelings and having them validated and witnessed helps to dissipate their intensity.

Triggers activate strong feelings. Our minds want to blame things outside of us and move away from these uncomfortable feelings as fast as possible. However, these feelings are inside and need to be outwardly expressed. Our grief is longing to be witnessed, supported, and nurtured.

Are you feeling things that are unexpected or that you have never felt before? We will take a deeper dive into feelings in the next chapter.

HEART WORK

- What triggers are you noticing? Write them down.

- Do you feel specific people in your life are letting you down?

- What actions would you like to put in place to better support yourself?

- Why is it important to take care of yourself now more than ever before?

CHAPTER 5

Feel the Feelings

"These feelings are just part of the nature of a human being. If you pay attention, you will see that they are not you; they are just something you're feeling and experiencing" (Singer 2007, 86).

Feelings can be pesky things. They can be uncomfortable, uncontrollable, messy, and embarrassing. As human beings, we are feeling beings. Yet we often repress our feelings and bottle them up. We tell ourselves we do not have time for them, or we want to appear like we have everything under control. Some of us do not like to show our vulnerability in front of others, or we do not know how to articulate what we feel. We have stuffed down our feelings so long we can't even recognize them anymore.

For too long, we have capitalized on happiness. Society shows us time and time again that any feelings other than happiness are to be avoided. "Happy" is the ultimate destination and symbol of success. I have found paradoxically we can only experience happy if we know the opposite. We can only experience the light if we have experienced the dark. We need to reframe pain as something not to be afraid of and moved away from as fast as possible but something to be felt and moved through. We enter this world with great agony and ecstasy. The journey of life itself holds the same extremes.

We need to befriend all our feelings. We need to get to know them intimately and become curious about them. By doing this, we gain the awareness of how feelings come and go; they are transient. Then again, sometimes they get stuck. To prevent grief getting stuck, it is best we allow those feelings to flow through us rather than run from or deny them. Repressed grief can manifest in a myriad of ways, for example illness or addiction.

The messages we commonly receive, like "stay busy" or "count your blessings," meant to comfort, only further inhibit the idea of slowing down and creating space to feel our feelings. Discomfort in this day and age alarms us. We have much comfort in our lives—warm homes, hot showers, soft beds, food delivered to us. When discomfort strikes, we immediately rush to change our state with a distraction like pouring a drink, scrolling social media, going shopping, or some other behavior.

When we experience grief, we feel out of control and search for theories and ideas to help us. Our minds will grasp to make sense of what has happened. We will find people or circumstances to blame. Our minds are powerful and will find all kinds of ways to avoid pain and grief.

RUNNING AWAY FROM FEELING GRIEF

After my mother died, I did not take a moment to feel my grief. I modeled what my mother had shown me after my father's death. I kept busy and carried on with life as if nothing had happened. Three weeks after her funeral, I went on a trip to Ibiza and partied the week away.

I returned to university to complete my final year. Then I made London my new home. I wanted everything new and nothing to remind me of the sadness in the past. I was twenty-one years old and determined not to let anything inhibit me from moving forward and embracing my new adult life. I got a job in fashion, which felt like perfect escapism from the darkness inside of me.

I masked my pain with the distractions of busy London life: work, parties, travel, relationships. My sister, Polly, had her first baby, my beautiful niece, Sabby, in 2008. Complications after a C-section left her fighting for her life. It was terrifying, but thankfully she recovered. While that was happening, I broke up with my then boyfriend. I was feeling terrible and eating constantly to try and ease the discomfort. More grief was accumulating.

I thought running a marathon would be the answer to my ever-expanding waistline and the weekends of drink and drug binges. I found out running was not the solution. I then decided my job must be the issue, so I left and started my own business. I poured all my attention into a luxury pre-owned fashion start-up and abandoned myself a little bit more in the process.

I was switching my addictions in an attempt to keep the difficult feelings at bay. Bessel van der Kolk highlights in his seminal book The Body Keeps the Score: "Traumatized people are often afraid of feeling" because they are afraid of being flooded by the pain and discomfort of the traumatic event. Van der Kolk explains, "It's not surprising that so many trauma survivors are compulsive eaters and drinkers, fear making love, and avoid many social activities. Their sensory world is largely off limits" (van der Kolk 2014, 249).

This resonated deeply. The food, drinking, drugs, relationships, work, and travel gave me temporary relief and a release from the undercurrents of suppressed negative feelings. I was unable to express my internal world in a conscious way. I could open up a little when drinking or taking drugs. Doing this was therapeutic in some sense until the depression the next day became impossible to cope with.

Understanding our emotional landscape is not straightforward for many of us. The first step is gaining awareness of feelings and then working out how to tend to them.

BECOME CONSCIOUS OF FEELINGS

Many of us initially understand grief as crying and feeling sad and think that's all there is to it. However, grief is a vast range of different feelings. In this chapter, we explore some of them.

As we work through grief, people are surprised by how many different feelings can be experienced in a short period of time. In my Conscious Grief Program, I give people a long list of feelings associated with grief and a link to a feelings wheel. (https://feelingswheel.com.)

At the beginning of each program, I create a text group on WhatsApp where we keep in contact between sessions. I ask each participant to check in daily with a feeling and a number to their group. For some people, this is the first time they have observed their feelings.

What is commonly expressed is how many different feelings can be experienced in one day.

It is not easy for most people to explain how they feel. It is easier to go into a story about what is happening around them. It takes practice to articulate what you are feeling. Many of us do not consciously sit and observe our internal feelings. The likelihood is you feel discomfort and unconsciously reach for a solution to change that feeling.

Practice becoming the observer of your feelings.

EXPRESSIONS OF GRIEF

Here is a list of words and expressions associated with grief:

Confusion

Disorganized

Disorientated

Restless

Impatient

Forgetful

Yearning

Longing

Overeating

Anxious

Fearful

Panic

Anger

Blame

Resentment
Rage
Jealousy
Frustration
Sadness
Spiraling
Lonely
Despairing
Excluded
Hurt
Depressed
Guilty
Regret
Changes in sleep patterns
Emptiness
Numb
Restlessness
Denial
Disbelief
Shock
Laughing
Drained
Exhausted
Impatience
Relief
Hate
Helplessness

Out of Control
Regretful
Weak
Lethargic
Forlorn
Defensive
Frustrated
Betrayed
Optimistic
Vulnerable
Apathetic
Powerless
Empty
Curious
Lost
Frustrated
Bitter
Annoyed
Stressed
Miserable
Thoughtful
Free
Worthless
Victimized
Impulsive
Snappy
Nauseous

SHOCK, DENIAL, NUMBING

In the early stages of grief, it is common to experience shock, denial, and numbness. Shock is a valid way for us to cope, as our psyche requires shock to be able to function.

The shock acts as a buffer against the intense pain, allowing us to gradually begin dealing with the traumatic occurrence. This is closely connected to denial. My father's death was sudden and unexpected, and I kept thinking, I will wake up and realize this was all a bad dream. My brain could not comprehend what had happened.

You might find yourself in a state of numbness, completely void of emotion. Maybe you are finding it impossible to listen to other people or take in new information. This reaction is normal. Our psyche takes time to understand what has happened. Dr. Alan D. Wolfelt says, "The mixture of shock, numbness, and disbelief acts as an anesthetic. The pain exists, but you may not experience it fully" (Wolfelt 2003, 49).

It is impossible to know how long you will remain in this place. We can get stuck here. For myself, it was a long time. It is a survival technique. However, the pain is there and eventually will require being felt and released.

CRYING
"Don't cry."

Since infancy, this is the message we have received. As adults, we feel shame when we cry, and we apologize quickly. We wipe tears away as fast as possible.

My German grandmother, Edith Nash, had to grieve the death of her only child, my dad. This was devastating, life crushing. Looking back, I have so much compassion for her. Edith was a private person, not someone who complained.

I don't think she could express the depth of her grief to anyone, which is heartbreaking. My sisters and I were too young and self-absorbed in our own lives to really consider her loss. When you are younger, you think the adults should have it all together. How differently I see things now!

When I was old enough to drive, I would visit her, and every time I was saying goodbye, she would begin to cry. I would sit back down and attempt to talk to her, but she was unable to express herself. It was difficult for me to know what to do. I would sit beside her and ask her questions to try and encourage her to talk, but she would never utter a word. Eventually, I would have to leave.

I have now learned from Bessel van der Kolk's work that there is a professional term for this called alexithymia, which is Greek for not having words for feelings (van der Kolk 2014, 115). Trauma survivors find it hard to describe what they are feeling. Some of us have to learn how to articulate what we are feeling. Physical ailments are what often alerts trauma survivors to their feelings. For example, back pain, headaches, or constipation could be signals of repressed emotions.

Tears are medicine. They have a soothing effect by releasing oxytocin, which relieves physical and emotional pain and lifts the mood (Murube 2009). Crying is a beautiful cleansing process and is healthy for us. As we become more comfortable with our feelings, we do not apologize for tears and wipe them away with embarrassment; we allow them to fall. I hope you will find yourself in the company of those people who welcome and accept your tears.

I will also add that if you do not cry, that is okay too. Not all of us emote in the same way.

TWO OPPOSING FEELINGS—
NO, YOU ARE NOT CRAZY

A common element of grief is having two opposing feelings at the same time. For example, you can be enjoying a social event, like a wedding, and feeling happy for the people getting married. At the same time, you may be sad because you will not get to share your own wedding with your parents.

After a few years, I was angry with my mother for dying. I felt like she did not try hard enough to live. I wondered if she'd had grandchildren, would that have given her more enthusiasm to stay here? It made me question that I was not enough of a reason for her to live. I dismissed these feelings and felt bad for having them. I thought to myself, How can I be angry with someone who is dead and not here to defend themselves? I decided being sad was acceptable, but being angry was not. I did not know back then that this is a normal reaction in grief. I was sad that she was no longer here, but I was also angry with her for not being here because I still needed her.

GUILT

I took David Kessler's Grief Certification Education Program and learned much about "guilt," which I am sharing as follows: (Kessler 2023).

- Guilt is a burden we carry. It weighs heavily on our minds and our hearts. We talk about grief "eating us up" as if it can consume our physicality. One of the ways we can help lighten this burden is by talking about it.
- Find a safe place to express your guilt. A skilled facilitator will help you reframe the story of guilt you are residing in. Our brains like to attach to this story because it prevents us from dropping down into the feeling. This is because we want to avoid the painful feelings.
- Underneath all the guilt is the powerlessness. Many of us don't want to admit to being powerless. Death is a natural part of life, and we do not know when it is our time to die. We have a predisposition that we should have a long life, that our children should out live us, and that bad things do not happen to us. If you are reading this book, you know that that is not the way life goes.
- When grieving the loss of a loved one, or a big unwanted change that has happened in our lives, we have a tendency to look back and analyze. What if I had done something differently; if only such and such had not happened; I wish I had done this; I wish I had done that, so that we could change the end result, so that we could have saved our loved ones from dying and saved ourselves from unwanted pain and change.
- These thoughts are normal; we are human; we are mortal beings who cannot control everything that happens. It is almost as if the guilt and the torturous thoughts of what if, if only, give us the sense that we are in this illusion of control—that we had a power to make the outcome different and that we think we can control life!
- In some ways, perhaps it is easier for us to feel guilty than to say that we were helpless, that there was nothing that

we could do because it feels more comfortable that we have some power to change things. Unfortunately, we do not have control over death. However, as much as we intellectually understand this, it does not stop the internal looping of the shoulda, woulda, coulda. So we punish ourselves.

- Some people you talk to will want to explain your guilt away, by dismissing it and suggesting you must not feel like this! Intellectually, you may know that it does not make sense to have this guilt, but that will not make it go away. You need to have the opportunity to express the guilt so that you can explain what you are experiencing. Slowly it will begin to soften.
- Understand that there are different types of guilt in grief.
  - *Survivor's Guilt*
    If you are a parent who has lost a child, the natural order of things should be that the parent dies before the child. Parents often feel survivor's guilt. Or maybe you were in an accident, you survived, and others did not. Perhaps you wish you had died and they had not.
  - *Relief Guilt*
    If you have been a caretaker of somebody who's been sick for a long time and they die, it is likely you will feel a sense of relief. You then feel guilty. Perhaps you feel like you cannot admit this to anyone. Remember you are not alone in feeling relief. Relief is a natural response in grief.
    I had a client who did not want to join a group because she was relieved her drug addict daughter had died. Her daughter had presented so many difficulties, and her death meant that she was finally free from the

ongoing pain. However, naturally, she still felt a great deal of sadness because this was her daughter.

– *Joy Guilt*

Maybe you have joy guilt, which is thinking that happy feelings are bad at a time of loss. When you find yourself smiling or laughing at something, you chastise yourself for having felt happy for a minute. Are you buying into the belief that you must not enjoy life because it would be disloyal to the person who has gone? Remember, it is normal to experience a range of feelings. If someone or something makes you feel joy and laughter, that is great! Give yourself a break from the pain of grief. You can feel joy and sadness at the same time.

When guilt and regret are present, be patient and offer yourself plenty of compassion. You may need to talk this out over and over again for the intensity to lessen. Looking back and reviewing what happened is a necessary part of grief. However, if the internal looping becomes unbearable, find help.

THE END OF GUILT

I interviewed Caro Brookings, whose mother died by suicide. Caro tried traditional therapy and grief groups and found nothing helped her release the guilt and looping thoughts. After the birth of her first daughter, the desire to end the generational curse of depression became her main focus, and she was determined to end the cycle for the sake of her new baby.

This is when she discovered NeuroCoaching, which rewires the brain. It had such a profound impact on Caro's life that she decided to become a certified NeuroCoach and help others using this modality.

Since then, Caro has designed the ASH method, which stands for Acknowledge, Surrender, and Harness Your Thoughts. This method uses a variety of techniques to help her clients let go of unhelpful thought patterns that are inhibiting them from finding peace and joy.

Caro works specifically with people who are grieving loss by suicide. You will find her details in the Resource Section.

ANGER

Anger acts as a defense against the vulnerable feelings of shame, hurt, and fear. When our lives are threatened by death or an unexpected life change, this can cause a surge in anger.

You might squash emotions that are deemed unacceptable. For example, in some cultural conditioning, it is not safe to express anger. "Nice, polite people do not get angry" can be the underlying belief in certain family systems.

According to "The List" that Louise Hay includes in her book You Can Heal Your Life, "Repressed anger is very likely to become depression if it has no outlet" (Hay 2005). It is important to be aware of when you are angry. Anger will often be channeled toward other people who have triggered us. Maybe those toxic bright siders will get the lashing of your tongue in the moment. Ultimately, we want to feel that anger in our bodies and release it in healthier ways than using other people as a punchbag and our tongues as weapons of destruction!

We need to acknowledge the anger and process it and then allow it to loosen into vulnerability.

Anger can be a transformational emotion. It can help take the lid off other emotions you are stuffing down. It can help move you into a new direction.

Do not be afraid of your anger: embrace it, feel it, and work with it. You will be amazed by what anger can show you. Please process anger in a conscious way by not hurting yourself or others.

IDEAS FOR MOVING THE ENERGY OF ANGER:
Free form writing
Screaming and shouting in the car with loud music on
Screaming and shouting at the ocean
Hitting pillows on your bed
Running
Shaking
Dancing to loud music
Breathwork class
Boxing
Grief Yoga

ANXIETY
Therapist, writer, and grief expert Claire Bidwell Smith published Anxiety: The Missing Stage of Grief: A

Revolutionary Approach to Understanding and Healing the Impact of Loss in 2018 right before the COVID pandemic. She could never have known her title would become universally required reading as everyone on the planet suddenly experienced some kind of anxiety.

Claire gives the definition of anxiety as "the fear of something real or imagined" (Bidwell Smith 2018, 19). Those of us who have experienced trauma and/or grief often go to the very worst-case scenario in any event, which is the fear of something imagined. It could also be an actual threat, like getting a diagnosis of being ill, or being in social situations. People can have anxiety, and they may never outwardly show it or express it because they know it is irrational, but the mind still plays havoc.

Claire remarks that the good news is anxiety is treatable. First, we have to understand what it is, name it, accept it is something we are grappling with, and practice rewiring the brain and behavior. Claire told me about the consequences of not consciously processing grief. "It's like that knock on the door, like hey, there's a lot going on inside of you, and when we don't address it, it bubbles up in all this anxiety."

See anxiety as a signal to begin consciously addressing your grief and finding someone to support you with this; more on this in the next chapter.

FEAR

When life changes in unexpected ways, it can leave us feeling fearful. We can flood our psyche with questions like What will happen next? Will I get unwell and die? Who will look after me? Will everyone else around me die? Will I be alone forever? Fear is similar to anxiety.

These thoughts are scary and make us feel vulnerable. Feelings of fear need to be expressed in a safe place. Much like guilt, family and friends might dismiss our fears and reassure us that there is nothing to be afraid of.

Place both hands on your heart, close your eyes, and take three deep breaths. Remind yourself, in this moment, you are safe.

FEELING SAFE TO EXPRESS YOUR FEELINGS

If you are finding the waves of emotion intense but you must maintain composure for work and family, I encourage you to "dose" your grief. In Conscious Grief Series 3, I interviewed Megan Hilluka, whose baby daughter, Aria, died in her cot at fifteen months old. Megan had two other children to look after, and she was pregnant with her fourth child.

Megan knew instinctively she needed time away from her young family to process her feelings. "I would ask a friend, can you watch my kids so I can go home and go through Aria's clothes and cry and grieve and really feel the emotions that I was feeling."

Megan talks about intentional grieving; she had therapy twice a week for over a year. It was hard work, but she knew this was the only way she would survive. This is what I mean about "dosing" grief. You dedicate time to feel. Megan now supports other grieving mothers about how to allow grief to flow through their bodies instead of repressing it. This is a representation of conscious grieving.

I hope you can find safe spaces to feel.

In later chapters, we look at how to support yourself when big feelings are present. One of the motivations for doing the work I do is my mother. I believe she repressed so much of her grief in an effort to be strong that this manifested as breast cancer. It is important to allow the feelings to be felt and for them to move through us.

Feeling the feelings is not always easy, which is why, in the next chapter, we explore therapies of various types that can support the tidal wave of big feelings.

HEART WORK

- Can you slow down and observe your feelings?

- Find a Feelings Wheel online. Write a feeling in your journal each morning as you wake up and before you go to sleep.

- Close your eyes and see if you can identify what sensations are happening in your body. Make a note of these in your journal.

- What feelings are dominating your days?

- Are you sharing how you are feeling with anyone?

CHAPTER 6

Therapies

"When we are no longer able to change a situation—just think of an incurable disease such as inoperable cancer—we are challenged to change ourselves" (Frankl 2004, 112).

In my early twenties, I was ashamed of going to see a psychotherapist. I kept it a secret, worried people would judge me for being messed up. I went to a few sessions but felt no affinity with the lady who sat nodding in silence in front of me. Five years later, a friend of mine suggested I try acupuncture. I was feeling exhausted and decided to try a session in the clinic where she was training.

Upon arrival, I was met by a giant buddha, water features, and calming music—a complete contrast to the designer shops below on Bond Street. The clinician explained to me that acupuncture can stir up strong emotions, and should I ever want to talk to someone, they had an in-house therapist. Internally, I dismissed it and thought, Been there, done that, didn't help. I don't need to speak to anyone, thank you very much!

I paid for several acupuncture sessions, and during that time, I experienced another tumultuous boyfriend drama. My self-esteem was at rock bottom. My behavior around food was out of control. I was in a shame spiral. I decided perhaps I did need to see that in-house therapist after all! I met with Ann, a small Irish lady with white hair, probably in her seventies. In my first session, I felt like she could read my mind.

I remember her acknowledging that I had been holding so much pain inside. Using the analogy of callouses on the palms of our hands, Ann described how they build up to protect us, but then they start to become sore and problematic. Immediately, she identified my coping strategies: work, boys, booze, and food, but they were no longer working. I agreed.

Initially, I resented the cost of therapy. It felt self-indulgent. My mind darted back to my abandoned relationship with God and the church. Was that not a complimentary route to healing? I revisited church; it still did not resonate. I made the decision to prioritize this financial investment in my well-being. Remember, I am from England, and thankfully, the stigma around therapy is not what it was.

Therefore, I turned up to Ann's office diligently once a week to discuss my issues. In hindsight, those hours were often spent on more superficial situations in my life, like work problems. I was dipping into my childhood, but my mind was adept at avoidance, making it hard to chip through the tough layers. However, this was a start, and the barriers were coming down. I realized I could not "lone wolf" things any longer.

I was relieved to find a therapist I trusted and enjoyed seeing. Ann set me on a path. She encouraged me to try yoga and introduced me to the brilliant work of Clearmind International. When Ann felt she had helped me as much as she could, she referred me to another therapist. For me, this illustrated her level of wisdom and integrity.

I was not being educated about grief and trauma per se at this time. Grief is not necessarily a genre that every therapist is well versed in. Consider this when choosing whom to work with. Grief is an experiential learning. While our grief is always unique and we cannot compare to others, living through certain situations can help us relate on a deeper level.

You might choose to work with someone who has experienced a similar grief to you. Are you ready to give yourself permission to seek therapy and invest in your healing? To help integrate your grief, many types of therapy can be supportive. In this chapter, I mention a handful. Finding personal recommendations for therapists of all kinds is recommended. When this is not possible, trust your intuition and see how you feel in the presence of someone you are considering working with. You will know when you have found a match.

Conscious Grief is a holistic experience—emotional, mental, physical, and spiritual. It makes sense to attend to our grieving hearts in the same way. In this chapter, I have broken down the therapies accordingly.

MENTAL AND EMOTIONAL
PSYCHOTHERAPY

Someone I wish I had met years ago is Mandy Gosling. Mandy is an accredited psychotherapist, researcher, and author specializing in unresolved grief experienced by adults and couples who were bereaved as children.

When I interviewed Mandy, she commented that it is common for conscious grieving to be delayed until decades after the death of a parent. If this grief speaks to you, you can find more information and resources on Mandy's ABC website listed in the Resource Section.

Finding therapists like Mandy whose practice focuses on the same loss you are grieving can be highly beneficial.

If you are grieving the loss of a spouse, sibling, or child, search for a licensed psychotherapist specific to your grief. You will save yourself time and money.

FORGIVENESS

We talked about guilt in the previous chapter. In grief, there can be a lot of negative self-talk and self-blame. You can also feel a great deal of anger and blame toward the person whom you are grieving. I held irrational anger at my parents for leaving me. I needed to process that.

The word forgiveness initially conjures up forgiving someone else. However, we also need to apply self-forgiveness. Remember, most of us are trying our best with the knowledge and skills we have available. If you are beating yourself up and holding yourself responsible for things beyond your control, you need to practice self-forgiveness.

Bring yourself back to your inner child and hold yourself gently and with compassion. If this feels relevant for you, I advise processing it with a coach or therapist.

EDU-THERAPY

I trained with Carole Henderson in Edu-Therapy which is a Cognitive Behavioral Process. This program comprehensibly educates the participant about grief and uses a step-by-step approach toward grief resolution. For people who want to work with intentional focus on grief that is recent or long in the past, this eight-week program offers deep insights and relief from stuck trauma.

Carole says, "I have been working with grief for over a decade and have always looked for how I could do better. I was thrilled when I found Edu-Therapy in Canada as it is so gentle and effective for all forms of grief. It inspired me to bring it to the UK as soon as I could."

GRIEF RECOVERY METHOD

I interviewed Nesreen Ahmed, founder of Harbor Light Coaching, in Conscious Grief Series 2. Nesreen experienced the death of her sister and worked with a therapist, which she did not find helpful. In fact, she found the process of talking about the death of her sister made her feel worse after each session. Things really started to shift for her when she found a coach that specialized in the Grief Recovery Method.

The Grief Recovery Method was founded in the 1970s by John James and Russel Friedman. The method leads people through an intentional process to look at their grief and the person, pet, or situation they are grieving from different angles. You will find a degree of commitment to do the work: required reading and homework is set. This method is action-orientated, addresses trauma and PTSD, and is designed to be done with at least one other person or in a group. For more information, visit the Resource Section of this book.

GROUPS

Listening to others and having our grief witnessed is a powerful part of healing. When my therapist, Ann, first suggested I do some group work, I was absolutely horrified! My initial internal reaction was I would never air my dirty laundry in public. Then I thought, Oh no, she thinks I am a total f**k up and feels unable to help me anymore, which is why she is suggesting group work!

I let my defenses settle and curiosity creep in. Upon Ann's guidance, I enrolled in a two-day workshop, "The Awakening" by Clearmind.com. This was terrifying to start with, but something about the group experience cracked me open in a way that individual therapy sessions were unable to do. This group dynamic was the loosening of the tightly screwed faucet on my grief. I cried my heart out for two solid days. Seeing and hearing the raw honesty and vulnerability of others assisted my healing process.

Being part of a group brings a sense of relief that we are not alone in our conflicting and painful feelings. By reading this book now, you are part of a group. Imagine—someone somewhere else in the world might be reading these words at the same time as you. We are never alone.

As a result, I created the Conscious Grief Program, which is an eleven-week group course. I take a maximum of five people per group so each participant gets the opportunity to share in every session. On enrollment, I speak to every individual and learn about their situation. I then have enough information to place them with others they will relate to.

Personally, I am reluctant to put my hand up and step forward in a big group! A smaller number of people creates intimacy and safety. By the end of the program, everyone has a good sense of each other's personality, process, and the person they are grieving.

My hope is that new friendships are formed by the end of the program and the support will continue after the group has come to completion.

EYE MOVEMENT DESENSITIZATION AND REPROCESSING

Commonly referred to as EMDR, this is a therapeutic method that helps individuals process, heal, and restore adverse and traumatic experiences. In this modality, we are titrating between the past, present, and future in a safe way, integrating movements as a way to stimulate the left and right side of the brain as well as bringing awareness to the thoughts, emotions, and physical sensations.

In Conscious Grief Series 3, I interviewed Beth Segaloff, whose partner, Ben, died while serving in Afghanistan. On receiving this news, she went to her closet and sobbed her heart out. This devastating circumstance set Beth on an exploration to soothe her grieving heart.

The closet was a trigger for her. Sessions with an EMDR therapist helped Beth work through this. Social Worker Beth found EMDR so effective she trained in this form of therapy and now uses it with her clients in her multi-layered approach.

EMDR in conjunction with talk therapy and other modalities creates a powerful process that can bring about profound shifts in one's well-being.

EMOTIONAL FREEDOM TECHNIQUE

Emotional Freedom Technique is often referred to as "tapping" or EFT and was created by Gary Craig in 1995. This technique is an effective way of identifying feelings and clearing them. The tapping is done on certain meridian points of the body that activate energy flow.

Due to the nature of grief getting stuck in our bodies, this can be a helpful tool to keep the energy moving. Naming the feelings also helps create awareness of what we are experiencing instead of numbing or repressing.

I spoke to Quantum Soul Coach Christina de Stael for my Wellness Wednesdays series on YouTube (Nash 2022). Christina explains that when the meridian points are being activated by the tapping, the cells are being spoken to quantumly. This calms the central nervous system and allows you to drop down into the heart.

Our mind often creates more suffering. Through doing a practice like EFT, we are able to gradually allow ourselves to release the pain and restore a sense of wholeness while remembering our loved ones.

PHYSICAL

Have you noticed aches and pains, headaches, teeth grinding, high blood pressure, ulcers? These things are signs of stress that need attending to. Emotions are stored in the body and become toxic unless consciously addressed.

In the New York Times bestseller The Body Keeps the Score: Brain, Mind, and Body in the Transformation of Trauma, Bessel van der Kolk explains how Western medicine has long ignored the relationship between body and mind. Countries like China and India have always diagnosed in a holistic way, and we are now becoming more aware of this in the West (van der Kolk 2014, 89).

Grief is highly stressful, and stress affects our immune system. Whenever we are in a state of crisis, the body produces adrenalin to help us react quickly and effectively, but the constant production of adrenalin lowers our immunity. Emotions like sadness, fear, anger, jealousy, powerlessness, frustration, and confusion will weaken the body. Repressed emotions, isolation, and a lack of joy and fun also affect our immunity.

Here are ways to decrease grief's impact on our bodies.

YOGA—WHEN YOU ARE STUCK, MOVE YOUR SPINE

Yoga is a good starting place to move the energy of grief. By stretching and opening the body, it releases stuck emotions. The word Yoga is derived from the Sanskrit root Yuj, meaning "to join" or "to yoke" or "to unite" (Yogapedia 2020). Yoga is connection, and grief is the opposite; grief is disconnection. We are disconnected from someone and overwhelmed by our process.

Yoga has been a steady supportive thread since my early thirties. I never imagined I would become a yoga teacher, but somehow, teaching kept presenting itself to me. I interviewed my teacher trainer, Sat Siri, and asked her why the physical movement, postures, and chanting in Kundalini seemed to pull back more layers of my own grief. She said, "Through the movements in Kundalini, the lungs are activated, and the heart is being stretched open. The breath and movements work the lymphatic system by pumping the lymph glands." This links up with the Chinese medicine I come to later in the chapter.

The temptation in grief is to close the heart, to protect it from fear of more pain. In a sense, the contraction can make the heart easier to break. What we want to do is bring postures that expand the chest, keeping the heart open, keeping the flow of love running through us. This takes practice because we naturally want to recoil into self-protection.

Sat Siri comments that she will see students break into tears while they are in heart-opening extension postures like camel pose or cobra pose. The movements stir repressed emotions, which will allow things to flow and move.

GRIEF YOGA

A safe place for those dealing with loss is Grief Yoga. In Conscious Grief Series 2, I interviewed the creator of Grief Yoga, Paul Denniston. I felt so inspired by his work that I decided to take his training. In his book Healing Through Yoga, Transform Loss into Empowerment, Paul gives a brief synopsis of how he was running from his pain through alcohol, drugs, and food. He said, "I overate and became disconnected from the world so no one could see my sadness. I was ashamed of my feelings, and I felt like a failure" (Denniston 2022, 15).

After training in various forms of yoga, Paul decided to create the kind of class he would want to take while grieving. This became Grief Yoga, and now Paul trains people all over the world in this method.

His intention with this class is to create a ritual that transforms pain and suffering into fuel for healing. He says, "What if we moved with grief instead of running away? What if we gave our grief the space to breathe and also honored our resilience and courage? What if we used the anger and grief to help us find more purpose, love, and meaning?"

Paul encourages the outpouring of anger, and also encourages engaging in joy and laughter. The reason for this is to give the individual some respite from their pain, teaching us that we can still laugh while we grieve. Laughter helps transition from heavier emotions and raises the vibration toward the surrendering and relaxation part of the class.

One of the most powerful postures is raising your arms in a gesture of questioning and repeating the question Why? Paul states that grievers have a primal need to ask why. Why me, why them, why is this happening to me? We feel affronted in our pain, like we have suffered a big injustice. It is okay to express that. Paul creates space for this in his class.

The mission statement for Grief Yoga is "To use yoga, movement, breath, and sound to release pain and suffering and connect back to love" (Denniston 2021, 20). This is exactly what happens when we move out of our thinking minds and become connected within. Whether that is a Grief Yoga, Kundalini, or Hatha Vinyasa, it ultimately brings the individual to a state of connection and restores a sense of peace.

BREATHWORK

When we grieve, our breath is shallow, which means we get less oxygen; this impacts our thoughts. The quality of our breathing impacts us physiologically and mentally. Many types of breathwork classes and techniques are available. You can begin simply with deep belly breathing. Check that you are breathing correctly. As you inhale, your belly expands; exhale and the air is pushed out.

Receiving more oxygen into the blood helps with stress relief, anxiety, depression, trauma, creative blocks, and detoxification. Oxygen alkalizes the blood, increases mood elevation, mental clarity, and pain management. The simple act of intentional breathing can have extraordinary benefits.

In Conscious Grief Series 2, I interviewed Jason Amoroso, who created Revelation Breathwork. This is an active two-step breathing technique. The same breath is repeated over and over again while listening to a curated play list and being supported by a facilitator. There is a buildup in the speed of the music, and one song is dedicated to the release known as the primal scream. Participants are asked to engage their voice, let out a scream, a cry, maybe it will be a laugh, but allow some sound to come forward.

This intentional opportunity for a vocal release is cathartic. Many of us were not raised to emote anger or scream, so this can be hard to do at first.

Jason explains how we store a great deal of emotional baggage and likens our emotional well-being to dental hygiene. "You brush your teeth every day or floss as a daily cleansing ritual. And if you don't, it builds up over time and you can have problems. It's the same energetically with us."

Jason says this technique can be helpful for people who struggle to meditate. Focusing on the breath helps the participant get out of their head and into their body. The breath also connects to the limbic part of the brain, where memories and emotions are stored. For those of us who like to be contained, this technique allows a loosening of the cap of our emotions.

This is why connecting with the body through movement, breath, and sound is exceptionally important. I incorporate a session of Grief Yoga and breathwork as part of the

Conscious Grief Program. I have found that participants who do not drop down into their emotions during speaking sessions find the postures in Grief Yoga or breathwork will invite a different opening.

One of the benefits about virtual classes and doing this practice from the comfort of your own home is not having to listen and witness the release of others. I know when I have done breathwork in a room full of people, I found it harder to stay in my process because of the outpouring of sounds and emotions in the room. With Zoom classes now available, you can be home, on your bed, and remain in your own experience.

COLD WATER THERAPY

The Wim Hof Method is one of the most prolific breathwork techniques available at present. Wim Hof came to his life's work after his beloved wife took her own life. He found solace from his grief and deep pain in freezing cold water. He explains that in cold water, his pain was silenced because the brain only thinks about survival (Wim Hof 2020, 97). This method has been scientifically proven to significantly reduce depressive symptoms (Touskova et al. 2022).

Personally, jumping in an ice bath sounds stressful to me, but I can identify that the long-term effects of this outweigh the initial discomfort. We can liken this to grief. If we dive right in and grieve with intention instead of avoiding the discomfort, the long-term effects are likely going to be easier to deal with than if we repress our grief.

The Wim Hof Method is based on three pillars: breathing, cold therapy, and commitment (Hof 2023.) I am not suggesting this method is for everyone, but I do know that many people find cold water therapy incredibly helpful. I find it compelling that his life's work came from the grief of losing his beloved wife.

CHINESE MEDICINE AND QIGONG

I interviewed Katie Brindle, Chinese medicine practitioner and the founder of the Hayo'u Method for Conscious Grief Series 1. Katie's enthusiasm and knowledge of Chinese medicine is contagious. It is fascinating what we can learn from this Eastern system when it comes to grief.

Katie has personally experienced grief in many forms. She was in a car crash in her early twenties, which meant she lost her career and ambition as an opera singer. This loss was followed by the death of her mother, who had been suffering with cancer for a prolonged time. After the birth of Katie's first child, she was unable to conceive again, which led to a long and complex fertility journey, adding more layers of grief.

First and foremost, Katie shares that the Taoist masters say grief is one of the most difficult emotions to process in the human body. Wow, one of the most difficult emotions to process. Let that sink in. This ancient medicine defines it as such, and in our modern society, we barely acknowledge it!

In Chinese medicine, grief is aligned to the lung energy. When a practitioner observes a grieving person, he or she can be hunched over, take shallow breaths, find it hard to finish sentences, and quite often have pale skin. Along with this, the person may find it hard to have bowel movements because it affects the lower colon.

Katie describes how grief affects the immune system, and this is why it is important to move the energy of grief. One way of doing this is by drumming the chest with your fists, which is a primal natural reaction. The Qigong Katie teaches has multiple exercises that help clear blocked energy and keep the qi moving, which, in turn, create healthy, happy organs.

The interview concludes with Katie's compelling words. "It is about allowing the heart, which is held in the lungs, to start to love again." A powerful reason of why we need to consciously grieve. We need to release it in multiple ways because if we don't, we shut down our hearts. We become fearful to love because the pain of loss can be so excruciating.

We are here to experience love, and grief can inhibit that desire. We must be aware of this and with it consciously, to keep us open to the wonderment of life. Katie says when we are open to that, then the lungs can gasp with inspiration and newness, the opposite of the gasp of shock and sadness. When we practice letting go of the grief, we create space. If your internal cup or your lungs are full of grief, mourning, retrospection, or looking backward, nothing new can come in, because it is full.

Embodying grief is significant. I encourage you to find your own interpretation of this. Perhaps it is running, dancing, walking, or hiking for you. The message is this: Stay connected to your body. Take care of your body while you are grieving. Do not abandon yourself in the process.

Grief will leave you feeling exhausted, and it will impact your body. Your self-care practice will additionally support your body as discussed in Chapter 2.

SPIRITUAL

INNER CHILD WORK

The recurring theme through these techniques is restoring peace and connecting with love. For me, personally, doing a daily inner child meditation was a transformative practice to develop a kind and nurturing voice within.

I facilitate Inner Child Meditations, which can be up to thirty minutes long. This guided meditation takes the participants on a journey to connect with the little you inside. So often in grief, a person has the propensity to abandon themselves. We need to actively seek ways to stay connected within and see ourselves and our lives as valuable and deserving of our own love.

Find a photo of yourself when you were younger and place it on your bedside table. Take a look at this photo each day and connect with the little you who needs your kind and compassionate support right now.

REIKI

Reiki is a Japanese form of energy healing where practitioners use a technique called palm healing or hands-on healing through which a universal energy is said to be transferred through the palms of the practitioner to the patient in order to encourage emotional or physical healing.

I interviewed Reiki practitioner Sydney Richdale, who says she can feel energy blockages or places in the body where people are holding pain. She is able to focus on those areas and break up those energy blocks. Sometimes there is a little more pain before the energy can be completely released, but this is part of the healing. Sydney describes the treatment like a "soothing gift for the body" and reminds us of the intelligence of the body. If we have pain somewhere, we have information of what we need to tend to.

SPIRITUAL PSYCHOLOGY

I received my master's degree in Spiritual Psychology at the University of Santa Monica in California and began my exploration into the grieving process. Drs. Ron and Mary Hulnick are founding faculty of the University of Santa Monica, having created and designed the two-year master's program in Spiritual Psychology in 1981. The premise of this teaching is that we are spiritual beings having a human experience, and that this planet we live on is a school for our souls' growth and evolution.

The word psyche means breath and soul. In the Western study of psychology, it is focused only on the mind and behavior. Somehow, the spiritual aspect got lost from the original translation, but Drs. Mary and Ron Hulnick have reintegrated it through their teachings, which they define as the practice of Conscious Awakening.

When we are babies, we are pure love. Life happens, we grow barriers to protect ourselves, and we become separated from our true nature. Their teaching provides a framework to reconnect with our true essence as compassionate and loving beings.

Our soul has many lifetimes. We choose the parents we want to incarnate through and the life lessons we would like to work on. This might seem a little far out if you have never heard this concept before. Why would some of us choose lifetimes of pain and suffering? Perhaps your soul is ready for high level learning and growth.

I find this to be an empowering concept. On a soul level, I chose to have this abandonment of my parents leaving early in my life. Now it is up to me to make meaning of that and learn what I can from it. Life is a school, and our obstacles can be seen as opportunities for growth and evolution. The premise is that life is happening for us, not against us.

When we stay open and curious to our grief, we can begin to observe our process. This helps to pull us out of the victim position of why me? I always like to reiterate that the victim position can be a very important experience to have. We need to be there and feel the sorrow and discomfort and not discount our experience. It does not serve to bypass the hard emotions. It also does not serve us to remain in the victim position, having not healed the material that has surfaced.

During this time of studying spiritual psychology, my conscious grieving truly began. I started to gain the awareness of how the grief in my life had shaped me. I began to reconnect with parents. Up until that point, I had put my grief and parents in a box. During this time is when I opened that box and examined the life I had chosen.

When you are ready, with perspective and time, you will see how this situation has shaped you.

The therapies shared in this chapter are a handful of ideas. I hope you can see how a variety of sources can help you while you grieve. You are worthy of investing in your well-being and personal growth. Try something new and stay curious as you explore modalities of healing.

HEART WORK

- Do you feel resistance about reaching out and getting support?

- Do any of the therapies I have laid out here appeal to you?

- What resources are you using right now to support your grieving process?

- Do you need to practice self-forgiveness?

TRANSFORMATION

CHAPTER 7

Modern Mourning

"If we mourn well, we live well and we love well" (Wolfelt 2020).

We live in a mourning-avoidant culture, which makes it easy to bypass the outward expression of grief. Bring back mourning, I say! You are experiencing one of the most challenging and devastating things that has happened in your life, and society makes us feel like we should just carry on as normal.

The distinction between grief and mourning is often misunderstood. Grief is internal, and mourning is external. Mourning is sharing our grief with others, which is why being part of a grief group community is an active way of mourning your loss. Finding unique ways to mourn loved ones helps create a foundation to integrate grief.

Traditionally, a funeral is the occasion that we devote to mourning. We rally around to organize a ritual that will honor our loved ones; we are consumed with making decisions on giving them a beautiful ceremony. On the day of the funeral, we gather with friends and family, we are in community, and we cry together and share stories of the person who has passed away. Once the funeral is over, people continue with their lives, and we are expected to do the same. However, the funeral is just the start. Most of us are still in a state of shock and denial at this time.

Our family had no road map for grief or mourning. After the funeral, the obvious reference point was to visit the place where they were buried or their ashes scattered. This place is a sacred space where you can remember and honor them. My father's ashes were buried in a graveyard a short walk from my nanny and grandad's house. Nanny diligently looked after the plaque and laid flowers on the grave of her only child.

During my childhood, occasionally I would visit the graveyard with my mum and sisters. I found it uncomfortable. I was unable to express myself in the way I wanted to. I could not wait to pass my driving test. My first trip would be to visit the graveyard so I could be with my dad and talk to him alone.

When my mother died, her body was buried in the local church near where she grew up. After her death, my life took a new direction. When we sold our family home, I was not concerned with keeping furniture, artwork, my mother's clothes, or jewelry. Emotional ties to material things felt meaningless. I was determined to leave the sadness and heaviness in the past. I compartmentalized my parents into that little box in my mind and shut the lid. My grief was isolated, private, and contained.

Years later, when my conscious grieving began while studying spiritual psychology, I wanted to open this box in my mind and remember my parents. I did not need to do this by visiting their graves. I could talk to their spirit or consciousness wherever I was. Another way of remembering them was through creative writing. I found a memoir group called Spirit of Story in Los Angeles. This provided an opportunity to write about my grief and my parents and share this with others in the group.

During the first lockdown of 2020, I returned back to England and lived with my sister, Polly. Thankfully, Polly preserved furniture and memorabilia from our family home, which I am now grateful for. I realize there is emotional significance to material objects, and they can provide meaningful connections to those who have died. Being in the surroundings of my sister's home, I had a desire to remember my parents through the lenses of their friends and family. I emailed cousins, work colleagues, and old friends of theirs and asked if they would be open to talk to me on Zoom and share their memories of my parents.

This experience was hugely satisfying and cathartic. Some people I barely knew graciously gave their time to talk to me and convey their memories. I felt closer to my parents, especially my father, who I have few memories of. This was an act of modern mourning. I decided to share some of my findings on an existing blog I had, the Chic Seeker, which was part of my fashion business and then it sporadically documents my transition to death and grieving. This outlet made me reflect and wonder how differently life might be if my parents were here. It made me miss them, it made me sad, but it also made me marvel at what they did in their short lives. They inspired me, and through this, I felt empowered in my grief (Nash 2020).

Witnessing people's reactions to this project of delving back into the past was interesting. I was challenged: Why are you doing this? I think it was almost puzzling after such a long time, and they questioned if it really was a healthy thing to drudge up the past. It was absolutely healthy for me. It created a newfound connection to my parents. It connected me more deeply to the feeling of love. It was like taking them out of that little box in my heart, hearing stories about them, and inviting them into my present-day life, which allowed more love for them to flourish in my heart.

You might get messages from people around you to not dwell on the past. This can, in fact, hinder our ability to grieve. By doing the work of mourning, which may feel hard at first, it does help move through grief. Be conscious that mourning will trigger uncomfortable feelings, remember your self-care practice, and ask for support when required.

A CONTINUED RELATIONSHIP

Dr. Therese A. Rando, author of How to Go on Living When Someone You Love Dies, notes that developing a new relationship with those who have passed is healthy. She writes, "Although death ends the life of the person you loved, it does not necessarily end your relationship" (Rando 1988, 233) This theory was published in 1988. It has taken a long while for these messages to filter through to become mainstream behavior.

Klass, Silverman, and Nickman wrote Continuing Bonds: New Understandings of Grief (Death Education, Aging and Health Care), which exemplified a paradigm shift that keeping a relationship with the deceased is indeed healthy and beneficial (Klass, Nickman, and Silverman 1996). Even though this is not new research, it still feels revolutionary because most people, myself included, tend to compartmentalize their grief. Talking and sharing about our loved ones can feel too painful. We might judge ourselves for being attention seeking. Due to the underlying belief systems to move on quickly and our discomfort talking about death, we do not have a culture that supports mourning or continuing bonds.

In order to grieve consciously, modern mourning keeps the memory of our loved ones alive. I wish I had another word for mourn because it sounds heavy! Mourning is a beautiful thing and can be light. We want to share about instrumental people in our lives. Modern mourning is weaving the memories into our day-to-day lives. This can be quirky and unique, just like you.

I interviewed author Jennifer E. Hale, who wrote Have a Good Mourning: 17 Ways Loss Can Lead to Inspiration, Hope and Joy. Jennifer's dear mother, Suzanne Hale, died of cancer, and Jennifer was lost in her grief. She tried the obvious: reading grief books, one-on-one grief therapy, joining grief Facebook groups, yet she felt like nothing was helping her. "They all seemed to only give me 'permission' to wallow in my sorrow for yet another day" (Hale 2020, 21). She felt trapped in her grief and was grasping for answers.

One day after her grief therapy session, she drove past a farm and saw a woman feeding goats, which looked like a fun thing to do! A few days later, she met with the farmer and found a new weekly commitment feeding sheep.

What she loved most was listening to the sheep chew their food! She said, "When I leave the barn, I am always on a sheep high!" (Hale 2020, 95). Jen's service of feeding sheep allowed her to take her mother's nurturing qualities and put them into practice. This act of service helped Jen honor her mother's memory. Most of all, it gave her the chance to find happiness again. This inspired her to discover other stories and write a book to promote mourning!

How do you plan on remembering your person who has died? Their lives and deaths have had a profound effect on ours. We can continue a relationship with them in a new form. Will you display more pictures of them around your house? Plant a tree or have a bench made with their name on it?

I hope this chapter gives you inspiration and permission to outwardly express your grief.

MOURN CREATIVELY

Author, journalist, and speaker Allison Gilbert wrote Passed and Present: Keeping Memories of Loved Ones Alive, which recognizes the importance of keeping continued connections with our loved ones who have passed. Allison noticed the opportunities for remembering her parents were mainly around the holidays and anniversaries, and she wanted to find ways to incorporate their memory in everyday life.

Thinking creatively, she found opportunities to talk about them in a casual and light way. For example, whenever they ate Chinese food, she would explain how much their grandmother loved dumplings. The result was, Allison says, "I felt closer to my parents, and my children were developing a stronger connection to their grandparents—even without having known them" (Gilbert 2016, xxvii).

In this book, Passed and Present, Allison finds eighty-five ways to remember our loved ones; some of them include repurposing jewelry, creating a scrapbook of memories, displaying post cards or letters with their handwriting in frames, and making playlists of their favorite music.

In my Conscious Grief Groups, the participants are invited to share photos of their loved ones who have passed. I dedicate a session to talking about the people who have passed, what their character was like, and what they did in their life. In this session, we let go of the story around how someone died and the suffering they might have endured. This is a chance to remember the life they lived and the impact they had. I encourage people to be completely honest and share traits that were not so positive. Everyone is human and no one is perfect.

This session is not an easy one, but it is an important one. It means the rest of the group gets to know our people, and it gives a context to the depth of the grief being shared in the group. In day-to-day life, talking about dead people can feel taboo, but this gives an opportunity to share without judgment in a loving space.

We explore ideas of how we can continue our relationship with our loved ones. Some people talk about cooking and recipes they will pass down to future generations. Some people bake cakes with their children on their deceased parents' birthdays. Others make tributes to them in nature. The possibilities are far-reaching.

One lovely participant, Becky Dawson, said that her siblings joked they needed bracelets saying "What Would Mum Do" instead of the "What Would Jesus Do." By the end of the course, she showed us that she had the bracelets made for herself and her siblings. Some months later, I received a package; Becky had sent me a bracelet with WWPD. Both my parents have the same initial, Penny and Peter. I was so touched. Thank you, Becky. Wearing the bracelet occasionally opens up a conversation. When people ask "What does that bracelet mean?" it is an opportunity to share about my parents.

WAYS TO CARRY OUR LOVED ONES WITH US

I created the opportunity for people to share ideas for how they were doing this in a Modern Mourning Masterclass. I have listed a few of the ideas; I hope this inspires you in some way.

- Sue keeps a heart-shaped locket with her husband Pete's ashes inside of it. She says how he is always in her heart.
- Hester lost a baby through miscarriage and said because of the nature of this loss, people tend not to acknowledge it, which feels so unsupportive. Hester asked her friends and family around the world to light a candle in

remembrance of her baby boy and then send her a photo or video of the candle. Hester felt like a child would have appreciated all the flickers of light from a candle, and the uniting in community to honor her son helped her say goodbye.

- Cathy's son died at eighteen years old. Many prayer cards were left over from the funeral. A friend of hers made jewelry from the prayer cards into beads. She made a necklace and bracelet for her and her husband to wear. Cathy likes to write messages to her son in the sand and take photos of them. She says she feels closer to heaven at the beach and therefore closer to her son. Cathy also likes to wear his clothes sometimes to feel closer to him. She says these things help, but the grief is still very painful.

- When Lucy's young daughter, Issa Ixchel, died, she asked friends and relatives to plant something in memory of her wherever they lived. A peach tree stands in her garden that she loved to sit under with Issa. Lucy started to write messages on ribbons and tie them to the tree and invited other friends and family to do the same. Lucy shared a ritual to help let go of the traumatic memories surrounding her death; she found pieces of wood that she was able to write on. She wrote down the traumatic circumstances that were haunting her on the pieces of wood and then she burned the wood in a stove. Once all the wood had turned into ashes, she buried the ashes in the ground and planted a bougainvillea tree. This ritual was effective for Lucy to let go of traumatic memories. If you are interested to learn more about Lucy and Issa Ixchel, please check the Resource Section for a link to her website.

- Joan shared about a ceremony that was hosted on Zoom. She was skeptical at first about how effective a Zoom ceremony could be. The celebrant who led the ceremony invited everyone to bring an item that reminded them of the person they were remembering. They shared their items; they were put into breakout rooms to share memories. She said they laughed and cried, and she was surprised at how healing the online ceremony felt.

RITUALS AND CEREMONIES

Due to the recent COVID-19 pandemic, many people were denied the opportunity to have funerals. A funeral is a ritual that helps our psyche to process grief and honor the person who has died. Without this ritual, the grieving process is impacted. So many people were unable to hug or properly commune with social distancing. It was just heartbreaking. The vision of Queen Elizabeth alone in the church after Prince Philip died is something that will stay with me forever. Sometimes we do not understand the importance of these ceremonies until we are deprived of them.

Ceremony and ritual are intuitive. You can create your very own rituals. There is no right way or wrong way to mourn: it can be a private affair, or you can share it with the world. Allow ideas to come to you.

The celebration of Day of the Dead in Mexico and All Souls Day in the Catholic church is something I wish we had in our national calendar in the UK. I think having a national day of mourning our ancestors and friends who have gone before us is beautiful. Why are we not celebrating the dead and remembering them?

In Mexico, it is a party, with street processions. People decorate the graveyards and share stories of their people in spirit. Death is woven and embraced into their culture. A ritual like this helps to dispel the fear around death and encourages open communication about this difficult part of life.

RAISING MONEY

A popular way of mourning might be doing a sponsored walk/run/swim for a charity related to the death of your loved one. This is an excellent way to invite your community in supporting you in such endeavors and connect with other people who might be experiencing a similar grief. Setting up charities or trusts in their memory and hosting fundraisers are other wonderful ways to mourn and support worthy causes.

When our mother died, we realized how many charities she was supporting. We decided to set up a charity in her name and called it the Penny West Charitable Trust. A year after she died, we hosted the Penny Ball and raised money for breast cancer research. We gathered many friends and business colleagues of our mothers' and honored her memory by raising money that will help other people. Sometimes our mourning can motivate us to create and help others, which is a beautiful thing.

ANNIVERSARIES AND BIRTHDAYS

The date of my father's death was a heavy day. We never created rituals or creative ways to integrate him into our lives.

So, when my mum died, I said to my sisters, "Let's make a point of celebrating her birthday." Every year, we make a reservation at a restaurant and get together. While we may not always feel celebratory or upbeat, we have honored this tradition, to take intentional time to be together to remember our mum doing something she would have enjoyed.

SOCIAL MEDIA

A great way to share your grief outwardly is through social media. It is lovely to see photos posted on Facebook timelines or Instagram feeds. This is a way to include your online community and give other people the opportunity to comment and message you.

On the twentieth anniversary of my mother's death, I decided to post a photo a day of my mum for twenty days on Instagram and Facebook. It was a wonderful process to find old photos and take the time to remember my mum, the things she enjoyed, and the memories we shared. Many of my friends never had the opportunity to meet my mum, so it gave them an understanding of who she was and the relationship we had.

Remember, everything in this book is an invitation; it is not a prescription of how to do grief. You may prefer to keep your grief private, and that is perfectly okay. Find what works for you. It might feel too soon or too triggering right now. Don't feel rushed, and it is never too late.

For me, the act of writing, reaching out to others, and having conversations helped to integrate my grief. It was a subtle transformation, a softening within my heart. Modern Mourning led me out of isolation and into connection. It can take a good dose of courage to do this in fear of being judged or upsetting others to talk about dead people. Only you know what feels appropriate for you.

HEART WORK

- Do you find it hard to share your grief outwardly?

- Do you feel resistance in finding ways to mourn?

- From reading this chapter, have you been inspired to get creative with how you mourn?

- Can you see how modern mourning can lead to less isolation and deeper connection?

CHAPTER 8

Gifts of Conscious Grief

"Someone I once loved gave me a box full of darkness. It took me years to understand this, too, was a gift" (Oliver 2006, 79).

Does this chapter title compel you to snap the book shut? It might feel like what you are going through is bereft of any gain. You ask, how can painful and tragic circumstances ever be wrapped up as a gift? Alternatively, the title might offer a glimmer of light in an otherwise bleak-looking future.

Grief can make us build thicker walls around our hearts. This is natural and understandable. We want to protect ourselves from more heartbreak, so building walls seems like a logical thing to do. In doing this, we repress grief, become harder, anger builds, and resentments surface. For a long time, I felt like a chunk of my heart went missing. I was trying to fill this hole with work, food, relationships, and so on. This physical, emotional, and spiritual hunger persisted until I began to consciously grieve.

Slowly but surely, I started to dismantle the barriers around my heart. This process did not happen overnight. It took time and intention. It still requires maintenance. Grief is not something that we get over, it is something we learn to live with, honor, and respect. For many years, I did not care if I was living or not. I did not hold my life with gratitude. I wrestled with it, wondering, what was the point of being here?

Just before my conscious grieving began, I had an unexpected wake-up call at Burning Man. I went to the dusty Nevada desert for the first time in 2015. I had been intrigued by this event; it is often described as life-changing and transformative. A temporary city of seventy thousand people is created for one week, and no money is exchanged; everything is gifted. People come from all over the world to have fun and revel in this human experiment of creativity. On the second to last day, I sat with my best friend, Emma, and discussed that nothing life-changing had happened. I declared I wanted to try some hallucinogenics, something I had not done before.

The universe provided, and later that day, I was offered DMT, or dimethyltryptamine. I had watched a documentary about this drug, and it was appealing to me because it activates your pineal gland, giving you an experience of how it feels when you die. I decided to try it, and it was the most intense experience of my life—and a scary one. I went to a very dark and lonely place, complete blackness. When I finally came out of the trip, I was exhausted. It felt like I had been on a roller coaster going off the side of the planet into darkness. I had to ground myself literally by getting on my hands and knees and touching the dusty earth. I have never been more relieved to be back in my normal reality.

For the first twenty-four hours, I was in a feeling of shock. It did not feel like the smartest thing to do. After integrating the experience, it became profound. The blackness, the nothingness, woke me up to the beauty of the planet I was living on. For my whole life, I had been taking my existence for granted. The awesomeness of nature became more vivid than ever before. This experience shook me and woke me up. I started to truly feel grateful for my life.

The use of psychedelics is being researched and used in professionally facilitated environments to assist depression and trauma. This is a topic for a whole different book. At this time, I was at a point when I still wanted to disassociate and was not satisfied with my reality. I felt called to share this story because it was transformative and the start of shifting my perspective on my life.

LEANING INTO GRATITUDE

I interviewed Susan Hannifin-MacNab, who was widowed suddenly at the age of thirty-eight. Her husband, Brent, died in a car accident, leaving her and her five-year-old son to navigate the grief and trauma that was now their reality.

"I was so angry, for so long," Susan admitted. Her outlet for the anger was to move her body. An avid fitness fanatic, Susan found refuge in running all over the city of San Diego. Susan owned her anger. "I was angry at Brent, I was angry at God, I was angry at couples I saw together who were my age and still married, and I would look at them with daggers." Being a pragmatic type who was in the field of helping others, Susan set about making plans to face grief head on and find resources to help her and her son. She thought, I can't live like this. I have so much heaviness, I have so much anxiety, I have so much despair, how am I going to move forward and get out of this and see some light?

First, she found a therapist for herself and her son. Then Susan booked herself on grief retreats. She tried meditation, yoga, art therapy, and breath work. Over time, she compiled a folder of the healing modalities she tried and neatly organized it alphabetically. This accompanied Susan to Camp Widow, a conference organized by Soaring Spirits International, where she presented her healing journey and all the things she did to support herself while she grieved. That was the audience that encouraged Susan to compile a book.

Seven years after Brent's death, Susan successfully published The A to Z Healing Toolbox: A Practical Guide for Navigating Grief and Trauma with Intention. The book includes twenty-six healing modalities ranging from animals, massage, and meditation to breath work. She incorporates stories of how the modalities helped her, her son, and other people who were also navigating grief and trauma. It is inspiring to listen to Susan and how the educator and social worker in her encouraged her to be creative (Hannifin-MacNab 2017).

I asked her what she found most challenging from her tools. Susan references the letter X, which stood for "examining your positives." She shared a story of a close friend suggesting she do a gratitude list. She was so incensed with this friend that she did not speak to her for a year!

Then Susan went to see the Dalai Lama, who was speaking at the University of San Diego about the power of gratitude, and her researcher brain decided to delve into how gratitude impacts the physiology of the body. Reluctantly, she started to write some things she was grateful for on sticky notes and put them in a jar.

A defining moment in her process was a trip to Mexico to donate Brent's clothes. While sitting on a dirt floor of someone's house with no indoor plumbing, Susan recognized she found a lot to be grateful for. "I am so thankful I have indoor plumbing. I have heat. I have a beach ten minutes from me. I have food. You know, that was a wake-up call!" The healing power of gratitude started to land for Susan.

Susan became a staff member for Soaring Spirits International, creating a new community of friends and support. She continued her private practice as a social worker and has launched a brilliant podcast. Susan is an exceptionally inspiring woman who exemplifies Conscious Grief.

Grief is a low vibrational frequency, and gratitude is a way to raise the vibration to help us feel better.

NEW FRIENDSHIPS
Being open and curious about your grief process means that you will begin reading books like this, maybe join a grief

group like my Conscious Grief Program, and meet other people who share your grief in common. When we talk about these most precious parts of ourselves, we create an intimacy that can go deeper than with old friends.

Find people who resonate with you. More grief communities have been created than ever before, and in this book, I have shared resources from which to choose. The most important thing is to look around and find a therapist, coach, and community that resonates with you. Listen to podcasts, find YouTube interviews, or attend free webinars from grief facilitators to help you get a feel for people with whom you resonate.

The new communities you find may not necessarily have a grief focus. Maybe you will find a yoga teacher whose energy you like, and you start to frequent those classes. Or you find an art class that becomes a community. If you create an intention that you are open to guidance, new opportunities will appear, and you will meet people who may never have come into your sphere if it had not been for grief.

I feel grateful for the work I do because I get to connect and meet with lovely people from all over the world—people with a willingness to share their hearts and have the courage to lean into their grief.

You may have found that unexpected people have already shown up for you. Some of those people may be good at loving. Some people will let you down. Some friendships you will let go of, and this will make space for new friendships to come in. Making new friendships that you would never have made otherwise is a gift of conscious grieving.

GRIEF AND LOVE

When I interviewed Paula Majeski for Conscious Grief Series 2, I joked that it was her fault I found myself in the death and grieving space. It felt like a wonderful full circle that I now got to interview her for the series. Paula is a multidimensional woman: a healer, an energy worker, an intuitive, and an artist. Her title reads "A Facilitator for Healing Consciousness," which depicts her work perfectly. During the interview, Paula reminded the listeners that we are on a soul journey, and we come to this earthly realm to learn and evolve. Some of us choose to come into this lifetime to experience great pain and loss.

Paula shares that one of the hardest parts of grief is that we do not have the reflection of love coming back to us from the people we miss. When our loved ones are gone, we have to find new places to share our loving. To begin, we can start by placing that love toward ourselves.

The soul part of us knows we are here to have whatever experiences are presented to us, but the human part is in the wrong or right. We feel like we have to give love in order to receive love. The human part of us misses the day-to-day connection, the phone calls, the time together.

Paula says it is okay to feel grief, but do not let it restrict your loving. She says there is a tendency to withhold and clam up, and this comes from the judgmental part of ourselves. The recommended thing to do would be to drop into your vulnerability and share. We can share by talking to others, writing, or creating music or art. Our soul is yearning for that because that is what returns us to a sense of connection. Helping others is part of evolution and growth because it helps move the energy and bring forward the loving.

Essentially, the message from Paula is to experience the depth of your grief to the depth that you loved. Learning to love yourself while you grieve is fundamental. If you can reach inside and give yourself the love you need when you are most vulnerable, this is a gift.

THE BEAUTY OF VULNERABILITY

If we choose to consciously grieve, our most painful experiences can soften us into more compassionate human beings.

Conscious Grief requires vulnerability. As Brené Brown teaches, vulnerability can indeed be a strength, not a weakness (Brown 2015, 37). If we respond to our pain with curiosity and openness, we can grow to be a more loving human being.

"Vulnerability is the birthplace of love, belonging, joy, courage, and creativity. It is the source of hope, empathy, accountability, and authenticity. If we want greater clarity in our purpose of deeper and more meaningful spiritual lives, vulnerability is the path" (Brown 2015, 35). What Brené Brown describes here is the essence of what it means to be aware of yourself as a divine being having a human experience. Can you allow conscious grieving to awaken you to who you really are?

Remember Ann, my Irish therapist? In a session with her, she quoted from the Bible and said, "Don't caste pearls in front of swine," (Matthew 7:6, NIV) meaning that the most precious parts of ourselves should only be shared with those we trust. This is important to remember: choose the friends, grief groups, or therapists who hold your vulnerability with reverence. When we begin opening our hearts and practicing vulnerability, we may feel like we need to divulge our full self to anyone who will listen. Be discerning, take your time.

Grief reveals our emotional depth. Feeling the feelings and observing the process teaches us about ourselves. This is experiential learning. Until you have experienced it for yourself, it is very hard to guide and listen to other people who are grieving. See this as a gift you can pay forward. Now you have the ability to hold the space for someone in your life in a new way.

SHARING YOUR VULNERABILITY

I interviewed therapist and author Sasha Bates. Sasha experienced the sudden and traumatic death of her dear husband, Bill Cashmore, in 2017. As a result, she wrote Languages of Loss: A Psychotherapist's Journey Through Grief. Sasha explained in our interview that her training in grief as a therapist could never prepare her for the enormity of being widowed. She found that grief is an experiential learning.

Her memoir is an honest account: gripping, deeply sad, and at times, entertaining. However, what stands out is Sasha is someone who is conscious about her grief, the feelings that come up, and her experience (Bates 2021). She does not have the support of close family, but her training as a therapist set her up with a wonderful community of friends who were able to hold a strong space for her emotions.

Sasha uses powerful imagery to help describe grief, which can be impossible to put into words. She points to different therapeutic theories and what she does and does not relate to (Bates 2021). An avid reader and researcher, Sasha made full use of her knowledge, and writing is clearly a form of therapy for her. She has written two additional books since 2019. Being of service to others by sharing our experience is a gift of Conscious Grief.

CHARITABLE ORGANIZATIONS AND ACTS OF SERVICE

Through death and grief, so many incredible charities have been created. The research and funding that many of these charities have provided have extended the lives of many more people. For example, Nancy G. Brinker founded the Susan G. Komen Foundation after her sister died of breast cancer at age thirty-six in 1980. The symbolic pink ribbon and breast cancer awareness month in October have become global phenomena, and this charity has raised billions for breast cancer research. The science and survival rates for breast cancer diagnosis have improved significantly since then, thanks to charities such as this.

You do not need to be actively volunteering with a charity to provide acts of service. It could be supporting someone on a Facebook post in a grief community. It might be praying for someone. It might be offering to pay for a stranger's coffee as an act of kindness. This has a ripple effect.

Volunteering or being of service can be an act of mourning that becomes a gift. Being of service provides purpose and community. I met Doryce Norwood, who attended the Conscious Grief Program after being widowed. Previous to being widowed, her daughter, Wendy, and ten-year-old granddaughter, Haley, were killed by a drunk driver. Young Haley's heart and other organs were donated, a gift of life to those who received them.

Her story is loss of magnitude. Doryce shares that being of service has been a lifeline for her. Doryce has been a board member of Helping Parents Heal since their conception in 2011 and provided pro bono legal counsel for this charity. She's also part of the Mothers Against Drink Driving (MADD) organization, providing support to others who have recently lost someone in the same way Wendy and Haley were killed. Doryce shows remarkable resilience.

RESILIENCE

Similarly to Doryce, resilience expert Dr. Lucy Hone tragically lost her twelve-year-old daughter Abby in a car accident. Her excellent TEDx talk succinctly outlines the three strategies she relied on to live with her grief (Hone 2019).

1. Resilient people understand that s**t happens in life. When tough scenarios occur, they understand that this is part of the human experience. Rather than dwell on "Why me?" they hold "Why not me?"
2. Resilient people choose where they put their attention. They focus on things they can change and accept the things they cannot change. Lucy focused on gratitude and found three things a day that she was grateful for.
3. Resilient people ask "Is what I am doing helping me or harming me?" This puts you in a position of control over your choices.

I think it is important to remember that it is not about bypassing the difficult emotions. Building resilience is a way to manage and dose your grief so it does not consume you.

CREATIVITY

"There is buried treasure waiting to be found in all of us" (Duncan Rogers 2015, 321).

I interviewed Jane Duncan Rogers, an award-winning coach, author, and speaker living in Scotland. The death of her husband, Philip, left Jane in deep grief. The expression of writing her journal became her sanctuary. Jane writes to Philip as a way to stay connected with him and track her progress. Over time and with perspective, Jane realized that grief taught her many things.

First and foremost, it encouraged her to accept "What Is, Is"—to experience the present moment, whatever it presented. In her book Gifted by Grief: A True Story of Cancer, Loss and Rebirth, she concludes resistance to what is happening tends to prolong pain, which then becomes suffering (Duncan Rogers 2015, 312).

The second gift was "Sitting Silently." Jane was encouraged to meditate by a Chinese doctor. The pain of her grief meant she was open to committing to meditation, something that she had not been able to maintain before. This practice awakened her connection of oneness "of love, consciousness, presence, God, whatever you want to call it" (Duncan Rogers 2015, 316).

The third gift she calls "Wild Wisdom." This explains how the death of Philip informed changes in the way she worked with clients. This new awareness was opening her creativity to new opportunities and ways of seeing the world. Jane was giving herself permission to be fully authentic in who she is.

Through her conscious grieving, Jane was able to reach a point of acceptance and gratitude for the death of her beloved husband. This was not to say that she would have traded all the wisdom for his life or that she no longer missed him. This new awareness was channeled into writing her book, that has transformed her career and life path.

From reading this chapter, I hope you can now see how, within Conscious Grief, you may find gifts. Everything we experience in our lifetime is in service to our evolution and growth. Keep reminding yourself of this and stay curious; ask yourself, What is this teaching me, and what can I teach others? Only then will you be able to mine the silver linings.

In summary, here are potential gifts of Conscious Grief:

- Gratitude
- Friendships (New)
- Vulnerability as Strength
- Deepening the Experience of Love and Life
- Developing Self-Love and Self-Care
- Being a Better Listener
- Becoming More Compassionate
- Seeking Transformation
- Growth
- Creativity
- Being of Service
- Resilience

HEART WORK

- Journal about gifts of grief. How do you feel about that terminology right now?

- Do you relate to any of the possible gifts in the list above?

- Have you made new friendships through your grieving process?

- Do you feel like you have a greater sense of compassion for other grievers?

- Are you willing to allow grief to be an unwanted teacher?

CHAPTER 9

The New You

"Real transformation begins when you embrace your problems as agents for growth" (Singer 2007, 81).

The death of a loved one is not something we will get over or recover from but something that forever changes us. However hard it may feel in the preliminary stages of grief, we have choices along the way about how we will allow this pain to shape us and inform the rest of our lives.

Whether you are grieving a death, divorce, illness, or massive lifestyle change, are you ready to acknowledge this is your new reality? Do you accept that pain and grief are parts of life? Since the pandemic, we have become familiar with the term the "new normal," so now you have to develop your "new normal" without your loved one or in your new position. It is not easy. We do not want the new normal; we long for things to be how they were, and this is why we need to keep processing what has happened.

When we experience a profound loss or change, it changes us. We are different now. Just as a tree loses its leaves in autumn, by the spring of the following year, the tree blossoms and begins to grow new leaves. In Conscious Grief, we go through a transformation. We may resist this. We may not feel like we have the energy or the inclination, but life continues, and so do we. This process is not easy. Sorry if I sound like a broken record, but being gentle and compassionate with yourself throughout is of paramount importance! We will continue to honor all of the feelings and then there will come a time when we want or decide to shift.

Studying spiritual psychology was a turning point, and I found a framework for my existence that made sense for me. I had resided in the Why me? and victim place, and this was of paramount importance to my healing. I had to accept the reality of the passing of my parents and return to those traumatic places. I applied love and healing to those places inside me that were still hurting. I allowed my grief to be witnessed. Then, through the teachings of spiritual psychology, I learned that on a soul level, I chose my parents and their untimely departure for my evolution and growth. This is a powerful teaching because it took me out of the wounded childhood and into an empowered adult.

My understanding changed that everything in life was happening in service to my evolution and growth. The obstacles in my life are there to teach me, not punish me. This gave me a learning orientation instead of feeling affronted by the challenges.

I am not saying I do not have down days or never feel sorry for myself anymore. It would be unnatural to not have those. However, I feel resounding freedom in the lesson that the challenges in my life were not presented to me because I was a bad person but actually because I was acquiring wisdom and developing compassion. The challenges and obstacles will continue because that is part of life. Now I choose to seize these as opportunities for learning and growth.

When I moved to Los Angeles to study, I did not know I would land on death and grieving, but I did have an intention to transition my career into conscious awakening in some way. My new self-identity was forming, and inspiration to work with people who were grieving began revealing itself to me. Becoming a group facilitator for the charity Our House was a poignant experience. I was facilitating a spouse loss group; it was heartbreaking but at the same time beautiful and heartwarming. I felt at home.

GRIEF IS FERTILE LAND FOR GROWTH

When I interviewed Transformation Coach Robert Pardi, he shared the wisdom that "grief is fertile land for growth." Robert was happily married to his beautiful wife, Desiree, who he met in college. Desiree was a doctor and a leading practitioner in palliative care. At thirty-one years old, Desiree was diagnosed with late-stage breast cancer. Robert became her caregiver and unknowingly her life coach for eleven years.

When Desiree passed away, Robert had accumulated a lot of knowledge through this experience. He missed caring for his beloved wife and being a supporter. He kept thinking, What would be an amazing story to come of this? He decided to leave his investment banking job, liberate himself from a lot of the unnecessary, and move to Italy. He learned Italian and gave himself the time and space to think, What is the gift I can give back? He is now an author of three books and helps people all over the world transform their pain into possibility. He inspires others to live an extraordinary life full of vitality.

Robert shared with me a quote that he and his wife used to say: "You can only live an extraordinary life when you value the ordinary moments." If death can teach you one thing, let it be that. We can get so caught up in the minutia of life. Small things disturb our peace until death comes. Then we look back and think, How did I sweat about so many small, insignificant things?

The human experience is not easy. We need the darkness to have light. We would not know happiness without sadness, or joy without pain. Sometimes we never appreciated how good things were or how charmed life was until we experienced a trauma that forever changed us. While we will never wish trauma or death on anyone to achieve this understanding, it is a part of the human experience and can deeply transform us if we allow it to.

LIFE IS NOW

Experiencing the brevity of life in my childhood made me acutely aware of how short life can be. If I have been unhappy in a situation, whether in a relationship or a job, once I have realized this is no longer serving me, I have made difficult and uncomfortable decisions to shift the gear in my life. The passing of my parents has given me courage. It has made me self-sufficient and given me a resilience that I may not have otherwise.

People often say, "What is your five-year plan?" I like to think, If I had two years left to live or five years left to live, what would I do? That snaps me into getting creative, into a reality of what is really, really important to me. Being aware of the impermanence of life encourages an appreciation for the present moment. The closer we are to death, the more alive we can potentially become.

Can your conscious grieving allow you to become more engaged with life?

Over time, a new you will emerge. It is like the grass growing. You cannot see it move, but one day you wake up and notice the change. You gain more peace. The anger has softened, the tears do not fall with such intensity, and the future is not so unfathomable. The numbness has lifted. New feelings arise. You awaken, more able to see the wonderment and awe of life.

POST TRAUMATIC GROWTH

More often than not, we all are familiar with post-traumatic stress disorder, or PTSD. The condition was first recognized in war veterans, but it is now acknowledged that a wide range of traumatic experiences can cause PTSD. In therapy, our issues are traced back to traumatic events that can give indications of why we have certain struggles in our present lives.

However, Post Traumatic Growth Research at the University of North Carolina at Charlotte is committed to the study of how some people can experience positive change as a result of a major life crisis or traumatic event (The University of North Carolina Research Group 2023).

Before delving more into this aspect of growth, it is important to clarify that just because individuals experience growth does not mean they do not suffer. Distress and grief are natural and healthy when traumatic events occur. Post Traumatic Growth does not imply trauma is a good thing. It is not. However, life can be difficult and often traumatic, and therefore, in many respects, we do have a choice about how we can respond. The Post Traumatic Growth will not apply to everyone as we are all unique and operating on different levels of consciousness.

If therapy is not committed to for long periods of time, it can hinder clients in reaching a stage where they can begin to identify growth from their traumatic experiences. Often, we stay stuck in our story, in a state of victimhood. I want to reiterate again here: Being in the victim state is necessary. In fact, it is a very important stage to be in for some time because we need to feel all the pain, the anger, and the resentment. I sometimes see facilitators or healing communities rushing people out of victimhood, and I want to say, "No, allow them to stay there!"

I want to say this largely because I avoided victimhood for so long, and that delayed my grief. It is important to be in that place, to reside in pain, anger, and the "why me." Then, when you are ready for a shift and ready to work on letting go of all the negativity, you can rise a victor. You will see the lessons and the evolution that is encapsulated in Post Traumatic Growth.

Five areas of Post Traumatic Growth can be remembered with the acronym OASIS (The University of North Carolina Research Group 2023).

1. **Opportunities**—some people will identify new opportunities that have come out of their traumatic circumstances that were not present before.
2. **Appreciation**—some may find a new sense of appreciation for life. They may have faced something so horrific the very simple things in life give them great joy.
3. **Strength**—coping and going through something beyond previous capabilities will give a renewed sense of courage in thinking, If I have lived through that, I can do anything.
4. **Intrapersonal Relationships**—some people find a greater sense of connection with those who suffer. Grief is a perfect example of this because we can relate to others in a way that we could not before a death or significant life-changing experience.
5. **Spirituality**—some individuals experience a deepening of their spiritual lives. However, this deepening can also involve a significant change in one's belief system.

When life proposes setbacks and challenges, we have a choice about how we respond. Can you ask yourself, what is this teaching me? How can I support myself while I am in this struggle? Who can I ask for help?

NEW YOU? YOU DECIDE.

When you go through a traumatic experience, like a death or a divorce, you will have your life before and your life after that defining moment. For me, 1990 was the year of BDD (before dad died) to ADD (after dad died). This was a defining moment in my life, like a slice through my childhood. Losing a parent at any age is a paradigm shift in your life.

I interviewed my friend Sami Fitz, whose father died in the first wave of the pandemic in London. Her grief was multilayered due to the COVID restrictions in place. After her father's death, the relationship with her sisters fell apart. Sami experienced nightmares for six months, ruminating on her father's death. What were his last words? Was anyone with him? Did he suffer?

Sami committed to Jungian therapy twice a week, read books about grief, and spoke with bereavement counselors. She says the grief was "too big" to manage alone. She described the effect of grief on her body. Her muscles felt tight. She knew she had to get moving. Sami turned to running and applied to run the London Marathon, which was a transformative experience for her.

Training for the London Marathon was emotional. She would think about her father and feel a stronger connection to him while running. One weekend, she was away with friends but still committed to her training schedule. It was a hot weekend in the summer of 2022, and she was in the countryside where there are plenty of hills. She had a breakdown and could not complete the practice run she had set out to do. She called a friend to come and collect her.

Sami felt angry and upset. Up until that point, she said she had been holding it all together. She felt safe to have a meltdown with these friends. One of them said to her, "I felt angry too." Both his parents had died by the time he was seventeen years old. Just hearing that, Sami thought, You know what? I am going to be okay. This moment of anger brought about a shift. On completing the marathon, her grief did not feel as big anymore.

Sami shared with me a dream she was having about a little girl wearing a white dress and burning down houses. The little girl became partly her, and they would hold hands. Then Sami became the little girl, and she was burning down the houses. This dream felt symbolic, like the anger was burning everything down so she could start something new.

Since her father died, Sami feels like she has grown up. She has become more in touch with what she wants and what goals she plans to achieve. She has gained clarity about how she wants to be treated by others. She had to reach rock bottom before she could build up from a solid foundation. She said she has learned to be resilient and to sit with difficult emotions. This is what grief taught her, and she says, "It is work when someone dies. I think you can shift toward growth. Then you're suddenly celebrating someone's life— the time you had with them—and grief becomes a process of surrendering to the cycles of nature instead."

Losing a parent at any age presents a shift and a growing up of sorts.

RESIST OR SHIFT?

Dr. Alan D. Wolfelt talks about the Six Needs of Mourning, and Need Six is "Developing a new self-identity, which can ignite resistance" (Wolfelt 2003, 75). You may feel like you do not want to be anything other than who you were before your person died. Feeling that way is completely natural and understandable.

You may resist the idea of moving forward and integrating your loss, but it is possible. Our most painful events bring us a wisdom, whether we like it or not. We have to decide if we will allow the events to teach us and help us grow. The manure from a horse nourishes the ground to help plants grow. Our shit—excuse the phrase—can be transformed into our wisdom and then it is something we can find gratitude for because it teaches us big things.

Your new identity might come with a label, like widow, widower, or orphan, which can feel uncomfortable in itself. The Helping Parents Heal community call themselves Shining Light Parents because they did not like the term bereaved parents. Perhaps widows and widowers could be known as Wisdom Keepers. In my mind, orphan conjures up this helpless image, but in contrast, we could be called Empowered Ones!

I met Kym Hynchey through my Tea with Tara community. I was deeply inspired by her story of profound shift and transformation.

Kym's son, Adrian, died, and in the same year, she became a widow. Kym shared that her life before these enormous losses was very busy. Her focus was on making money, and she kept people at a distance. She said, "I felt proud of myself for not getting emotionally affected by other people." Then grief struck her life, and everything changed. Overnight, Kym learned what was essential and what mattered. Everything she had previously striven for did not matter.

The loss in her life made her want to live with intention. Kym wanted to be authentic in every relationship because she realized she had been playing a character in her old life and was not being fully herself. The grief washed away the walls she had around her heart and left her vulnerable and soft. In her previous life, she would have seen that as weakness. Now she views this as a strength. Kym is now able to express her love for others and openly tell them.

Kym took David Kessler's Grief Educator program. At first, she was angry and devastated by the death of her son and husband, but during that training, she developed a profound awareness.

Kym thought, I have two choices. I can live remembering all the sadness and trauma that surrounded their deaths, or I can live with the memories of love and the profound relationships I had with my son and husband.

Kym decided to relocate to a new city with her living son; she had too many sad memories in her old home. Her career transitioned, and she created Adrian Grief Support, named after her late son. His life lives on through this legacy of her career as a grief coach supporting others with the tools and wisdom she has acquired.

Ultimately, everything in life is a story. You choose which religion or belief structure makes most sense to you. You choose whether this life is happening for you or against you. You get to choose what you want your story to be. So let this experience be your greatest teacher! Allow yourself to feel it all: be the victim, return to the child, tend to that little one who resides in you. With care, love, and nurturing, you can raise a new you. Then you can slowly rise, like a phoenix from the ashes, different now, having gained wisdom, insights, and deeper compassion for the human experience.

The Japanese practice of fixing broken pottery is called Kintsugi. The broken pieces are put back together using gold. In doing so, they become even more beautiful than they were before. Can you hold this vision for yourself? While you may feel far away from anything beautiful right now, it is possible for the cracks in your broken heart to be filled with gold. The gold has become the wisdom, the new connections, the creativity, and the depths of love you have felt because of your pain and the awareness that you are a divine being having a human experience. This gold will make you whole again.

HEART WORK

- Reflect on how this experience has changed you.

- Are you going to love the new version of yourself?

- How can you turn your pain into power for good?

- Can you let this experience open your heart and share more love with the world?

Conscious Grief

"Conscious Grief is conscious awakening."
—TARA NASH

I still grieve. I still have sorrow in my heart, but I accept that as a sacred part of me. It is not something to fear. Now that I am consciously aware of it, the sorrow brings a softening. My vulnerability fuels my compassion. Through conscious grieving, I have reached a place of gratitude for every loss and for every day I am alive.

Every moment provides lessons and wisdom. This does not negate the true human experience of longing and yearning and looking back and thinking, If only things could have been different. When I have a day of feeling sorry for myself, or my heart hurts, instead of reaching for pints of ice cream or liters of gin and tonic, I have equipped myself with tools and awareness to soothe myself consciously and restore peace and wholeness.

In the past, I was transfixed on the difficulties and pain in life. I thought I was hypervigilant, getting prepared for the next traumatic event to happen. I thought this was a safe place to reside. I was ready with my heart armor to protect myself from more pain. However, what was actually happening was my nervous system was on high alert and I was not living fully.

Through the intention of conscious grieving, I was no longer afraid of the pain but walked toward it. In doing this, I realized I gained greater freedom and expansion. I was living a contracted existence, and now I live from a place of spaciousness. I found that the more engaged I became in the full spectrum of all my feelings, the more connected I felt to the experience of being alive. My nervous system could relax and see the joy, experience more love, and finally feel true gratitude for my existence.

Conscious Grieving opened my heart and deepened my capacity to share my loving, to others and to myself. I hope you can hold this intention for yourself. Can you love yourself as you grieve? Can you hold your life with reverence and gratitude for all the pain and struggle it can bring? Know that you matter, your life matters, and you have a right to be here.

We are here on this earth to experience the polarities that the human experience brings. Everything in life is constantly shifting and moving. Can you trust that wherever you are right now in your experience, it will not stay like this forever? I know we want things to move at our own speed, and we want to control and manipulate our experience, but sometimes this is not possible. Grief will teach you that.

Use every obstacle as a catalyst for growth and transformation. Keep your heart open and keep asking "What is this teaching me?" We are not here to get stuck in the polarity of grief, pain, trauma, fear, and disconnection. We are here to find our way from the darkness and into the light.

From asking over eighty interview participants what their interpretation of Conscious Grief was, Gary Roe's explanation encapsulates it beautifully. "I think Conscious Grief is engaging with our losses, learning from our losses, and making the commitment to really heal and grow, which means to grieve in healthy ways. Stop running from grief, stop hiding from grief, and instead just exist with it."

It can be hard to drop into our pain and vulnerability. It can be hard to find places where that is welcome and accepted. This is why grief can be an isolating experience where we remain stuck. Many people and situations will require the sunny-side up version of yourself. I encourage you to find those communities and places where you can drop into your heart and authentically feel and express yourself. Befriend all the feelings, especially those we deem as negative. Find ways to sit with them and be present. Then find ways to transform them. It is possible.

The experience of death and grieving will change you. It could set your life in a whole new direction. It might alter the way you see the world and your existence. Can you allow yourself to stay open and curious to this process? Allow your grief to show you new ways of being?

As you tend to your grief consciously, can you develop self-care in new ways? How do you want to treat yourself as you walk this difficult path? Can you develop a kind and nurturing voice within?

Only you can set the intention on how to support your conscious grieving.

I personally believe that we heal best in community by having our grief witnessed because this brings connection with others. However, I know for other people, healing alone has been the most supportive.

It is never too late to begin grieving consciously. It took me decades. Sometimes we need to step back into the darkness in order to embrace those fragments of ourselves, to piece ourselves back together. When your consciousness is ready, it will be your responsibility to give yourself the time and space required for healing.

Healing is hard. Conscious Grief can be hard, but on the other side of pain is wonder, awe, rebirth, love, connection, and peace. The ripple effect of Conscious Grief can be enormous. Think about it: if we allow our pain to harden us, that does not lead to more open and loving people. Conscious Grief creates openness and more connected, loving, and compassionate beings, and that is what we need more of on the planet.

You have all the answers inside of you. Trust yourself to find the guidance you need. Take deep breaths, spend time in nature, find a moment of joy in each day, and write one thing down that you are grateful for every day. Reach out to someone and tell them you love and appreciate them.

To summarize Conscious Grief, here are the ten pillars for your tool kit.

TEN PILLARS OF CONSCIOUS GRIEF
1. Ask for help
2. Release feelings
3. Find community to witness your grief
4. Move your body
5. Develop a self-care plan
6. Ask What am I learning?
7. Be gentle and compassionate with yourself
8. Take responsibility for your healing
9. Implement creativity—journal, paint, knit, crochet, etc.
10. Offer daily gratitude

My intention in writing this book is to share some of what I have learned in my life up until now. It is also to share the work of some of the amazing people I have been fortunate to meet. I was approaching my forty-second birthday, the same age as when my father's life ended. He created an awful lot in his short life and left a legacy to be proud of. My hope is that if my life came to an end tomorrow, this book would go on to help others after I have gone.

However, since it has taken me over half my life to get to a point of gratitude for being here, I hope and pray for a long and healthy life. When I moved to Los Angeles to study spiritual psychology, I knew I wanted to transition my career from fashion. I was drawn to working in the field of helping others. It came as a surprise to me that I would land on grief. It seems so obvious to me now!

When I explain to people what I do, some people give me this sort of wincing facial expression. If I could read their minds, I'd imagine them thinking, That sounds low vibration or How depressing. What most people do not realize is that joy, laughter, and excitement absolutely do coexist with deep sadness and heartache. If you are consciously feeling it all, you are awake and relishing in the rollercoaster of the human experience.

If we are not dulling our senses and reminding ourselves to return to the present moment, we can find beauty and magic all around us. We choose which spectacles to view our human experiences through.

Have your grief, find your joy, move those emotions through you, and allow yourself to be transformed and softened.

You have felt love deeply, or else you would not be reading this book. That is a beautiful thing.

Acknowledgments

First and foremost, I would like to thank my sisters, Lisa and Polly, for their unwavering belief in me that I could write a book. I am so grateful for your friendship and support; I love you very much.

Thank you to all the people who said yes to being interviewed for the Conscious Grief Series. It has been an honor to sit with each of you and learn from your wisdom.

Thank you to the participants of the Conscious Grief Program and others who have trusted their hearts to sit with me in their grief.

I am beyond grateful for the amazing emails I received from people who subscribe to my newsletter and sent me messages of support and encouragement. You will never know how your words gave me the will to keep pushing forward.

Thank you to my friends who have encouraged and supported me during this process. Thank you for understanding when I have canceled and changed plans in an effort to keep my focus on getting this book finished. I am so grateful for the amazing friends I have in my life. You know who you are.

Thank you to my teachers and mentors: Ann Farley, Sadiye Stevens, Duane and Catherine O'Kane, Cheryl Fidelman, Drs. Mary and Ron Hulnick, Paula Majeski, Sat Siri, Paul Denniston, Jason Amoroso, Carole Henderson, Mandy Gosling, Elaine Mary Collins, Nicole Von Bredow, Patrice Kimmins, Karin Gutman, Mary Ann Tate, and Carol McKibben.

Thank you to Emma Cannon for sowing the initial seed to write this book. I got there eventually!

Thank you to my wordsmith extraordinaire witch, Clemmie Myers, who tapped the finishing touches like a fairy godmother. I am beyond grateful.

Lastly, thank you for Gods gifts—tea, coffee, chocolate, and my baby dog—to keep me going. Kenny spent many hours sitting on my lap as I typed away and gave me a reason to take a break and go for a walk.

Resources

These are mostly recommendations of people I have met and interviewed through the Conscious Grief Series. Some are based in the UK and some in the US, Canada, or Australia.

BEREAVED CHILDREN CHARITIES

Child Bereavement UK: https://www.childbereavementuk.org/
Good Grief USA: https://good-grief.org/
EmpoweringHer UK and USA:
    https://www.empoweringher.org/
Winstons Wish: https://www.winstonswish.org/

OTHER CHARITIES

James' Place—Men Suicide Prevention:
    https://www.jamesplace.org.uk/
Suicide Prevention UK: https://www.spuk.org.uk/
Mothers Against Drunk Driving: https://madd.org/
Susan G. Komen Foundation https://madd.org/
    https://www.komen.org/
Helping Parents Heal: https://www.helpingparentsheal.org/
Our House: https://www.ourhouse-grief.org/

CHILD LOSS

Helping Parents Heal: https://www.helpingparentsheal.org/
Megan Hilluka, Grieving Mom's Haven:
     https://www.meganhillukka.com/
Erics House: https://www.ericshouse.org/
Lucy Sessions: https://www.lucysessions.co.uk/grief-support.html

FERTILITY PROBLEMS

Emma Cannon: https://www.emmacannon.co.uk/

GETTING SOBER

Sara Perry: https://www.sparkjoycoaching.com/

GRIEF AND CREATIVITY

The Good Grief Project: https://thegoodgriefproject.co.uk/
Poetry: https://chanelbrenner.com/
Linda Broder: https://www.stringsofzen.com/

LIFE TRANSITIONS

Helene Stelian: https://www.helenetstelian.com/

MEDIUMS

Suzanne Giesemann: https://suzannegiesemann.com/
Melinda Vail: https://melindavail.com/
Kat B: https://www.kat-b.com/
Debbie Squizzero: https://www.debbiesquizzero.com/
Cate Coffelt: https://catecoffelt.com/

PET LOSS

Jackie Weaver: https://www.animalpsychic.co.uk/pet-grief
Marian Silverman: https://yourpetloss.com/
Liz Murdoch: https://talkingwiththedogs.com/

PREGNANCY AFTER LOSS
Tahnee Knowles: https://pregnancyafterlosssupport.org/

RELATIONSHIP GRIEF AND DIVORCE
Amanda Lambros: https://www.amandalambros.com/
Sara Davidson: https://www.saradavison.com/
Carrie Doubts: https://lifesnextchaptercoaching.com/
Cheryl Fidelman: https://cherylfidelman.com/

SELF-CARE
Polly Webb Nutrition: https://www.soundeating.co.uk/
Emma Ball Meditation:
    https://www.evolvehealingandmeditation.com/

SPIRITUAL GRIEF COACHING
Tara Nash: https://www.tara-nash.com/
Paula Majeski: https://www.paulamajeski.com/
Uma Girish: https://umagirish.com/
Meghan Smith Brooks: https://www.unravelinggrief.com/

SUICIDE LOSS BEREAVEMENT
Healing to the Max: https://healingtothemax.org/
Suicide Bereavement Coaching:
    https://suicidebereavementcoaching.com/

THERAPIES
Acupuncture: https://www.wendymandy.uk/
Acupuncture and Qigong: https://www.katiebrindle.com/
Adults Bereaved as Children, Mandy Gosling:
    https://abcgrief.co.uk/
A to Z Healing Toolbox: https://www.a2zhealingtoolbox.com/
Clearmind International: https://clearmind.com/

EFT: https://www.emofree.com/
Edu-Therapy: https://www.edu-therapy.uk/
Emma Cannon Author and Acupuncturist:
    https://www.emmacannon.co.uk/
EMDR: https://www.bethsegaloff.com/
Kym Hynchey Grief Coach: https://agriefsupport.com/
Nesreen Ahmed: https://harborlightcoaching.com/
Spiritual Psychology, University of Santa Monica:
    https://www.universityofsantamonica.edu/
The Grief Recovery Method:
    https://www.griefrecoverymethod.com/
Reiki: https://www.reiki.org/
Revelation Breathwork: https://www.revelationbreathwork.com/
Robert Pardi: https://www.robertpardi.com/
Spirit of Story: https://www.spiritofstory.com/
Wim Hof Breathwork: https://www.wimhofmethod.com/

YOGA

Sat Siri: https://satsiri.mykajabi.com/
Paul Denniston: https://griefyoga.com/
Emma Conally-Barklem: https://www.emmaliveyoga.com/

INSTAGRAM PAGES

Randi Wolfson @griefandgrits
Mark Lemon @marklemonofficial
Kayleigh O'Connor @goodgrief_uk
Sara Cobb @my_grief_connection
Sophie Mills @the_grief_revolution
Clemmie Myers Creatives @limegreenbow

Appendix

CHAPTER 1—GRIEF CONSCIOUSNESS

Edelman, Hope. 2021. The AfterGrief: Finding Your Way on the Long Path of Loss. UK: Penguin Random House.

Freud, Sigmund. 1964. Mourning and Melancholia—The Standard Edition of the Complete Psychological Works of Sigmund Freud, Vol. XIV (1914–1916). London: Hogarth Press.

James, John W., and Russell Friedman. 2009. The Grief Recovery Handbook: The Action Program for Moving Beyond Death, Divorce, and Other Losses including Health, Career, and Faith. New York: Harper Collins.

Kessler, David. 2023. "Grief Educator Certification with David Kessler." Grief.com. Accessed September 14, 2022. https://www.davidkesslertraining.com/certification.

Kübler-Ross, Elisabeth, MD. 1969. On Death and Dying: What the Dying Have to Teach Doctors, Nurses, Clergy and Their Own Families. New York City: Simon & Schuster.

Oxford Language Dictionary. Ninth Edition. 2006. Oxford: Oxford University Press.

CHAPTER 2—SELF-CARE

"Boundaries." 2018. LifeVersation (blog). October 24, 2018. https://www.lifeversation.com/blog/boundaries2149559.

Carroll, Laurina. 2022. "Ayurvedic Diet and Digestion." Your Ayurveda Consultant (blog). December 3, 2022. https://yourayurvedaconsultant.com/ayurvedic-diet-and-digestion/.

Didion, Joan. 2020. A Year of Magical Thinking. Read by Vanessa Redgrave. Newark: Audible Originals. Audio Books, 1:28.

Devine, Megan. 2017. It's OK That You're Not OK: Meeting Grief and Loss in a Culture That Doesn't Understand. Louisville, Colorado: Sounds True.

Nash, Tara. 2022. "Monday Mini Meditation." Conscious Grief. July 27, 2022. 6:06. https://www.youtube.com/watch?v=pgTtx-buWTA&t=231s.

Oxford Language Dictionary. Ninth Edition. 2006. Oxford: Oxford University Press.

Pinker, Susan. 2021. "Storytelling Makes Hearts Beat as One." The Wall Street Journal, October 9, 2021. https://www.wsj.com/articles/storytelling-makes-hearts-beat-as-one-11633795321.

Science Daily. 2007. "Getting Dirty May Lift Your Mood." April 10, 2007. https://www.sciencedaily.com/releases/2007/04/070402102001.htm.

Science Daily. 2019. "Stress Reduction Benefits from Petting Dogs, Cats." July 15, 2019. www.sciencedaily.com/releases/2019/07/190715114302.htm.

Seal, Rebecca. 2021. "Unlocking the Gut Microbiome'—and Its Massive Significance to Our Health." The Guardian, July 11, 2021. https://www.theguardian.com/society/2021/jul/11/unlocking-the-gut-microbiome-and-its-massive-significance-to-our-health.

Williams, Litsa. 2014. "Grief Theory 101: The Dual Process Model of Grief." What's Your Grief (blog). September 23, 2014. https://whatsyourgrief.com/dual-process-model-of-grief/.

CHAPTER 3—BELIEFS

Barks, Coleman, and John Moyne. 2004. The Essential Rumi. New York City: Harper One.

Campbell, Colin. 2023. Finding the Words. Working Through Profound Loss with Hope and Purpose. New York City: Penguin Random House.

Emoto, Dr. Masaru. 2005. The Hidden Messages in Water. New York City: Atria Books.

CHAPTER 4—TRIGGERS

Brenner, Chanel. 2014. Vanilla Milk: A Memoir Told in Poems. Los Angeles: Silver Birch Press.

Campbell, Colin. 2023. Finding the Words. Working Through Profound Loss with Hope and Purpose. New York City: Penguin Random House.

Pedersen, Traci. 2022. "What Are Triggers, and How Do They Form?" Psych Central (blog). April 28, 2022. https://psychcentral.com/lib/what-is-a-trigger#what-is-a-trigger.

Wolfelt, Alan D., PhD. 2003. Understanding Your Grief: Ten Essential Touchstones for Finding Hope and Healing Your Heart. Fort Collins, Colorado: Companion Press.

CHAPTER 5—FEEL THE FEELINGS

Bidwell Smith, Claire, LCPC. 2018. Anxiety: The Missing Stage of Grief: A Revolutionary Approach to Understanding and Healing the Impact of Loss. Boston: Da Capo Press.

Hay, Louise. 2005. You Can Heal Your Life. Carlsbad, California: Hay House.

Kessler, David. 2023. "Grief Educator Certification with David Kessler." Grief.com. Accessed September 14, 2022. https://www.davidkesslertraining.com/certification.

Murube, Juan. 2009. "Hypotheses on the Development of Psychoemotional Tearing." The Occular Surface vol. 7, no. 4 (October 2009): 171–175. https://www.sciencedirect.com/journal/the-ocular-surface/vol/7/issue/4.

Singer, Michael A. 2007. The Untethered Soul: The Journey Beyond Yourself. Oakland, California: New Harbinger Publications Inc.

Van der Kolk, Bessel. 2014. The Body Keeps the Score: Brain, Mind, and Body in the Transformation of Trauma. London: Penguin Random House UK.

Wolfelt, Alan D., PhD. 2003. Understanding Your Grief: Ten Essential Touchstones for Finding Hope and Healing Your Heart. Fort Collins, Colorado: Companion Press.

CHAPTER 6—THERAPIES

Denniston, Paul. 2022. Healing Through Yoga: Transform Loss into Empowerment with More than 75 Yoga Poses and Meditations. London: Chronicle Prism UK.

Frankl, Viktor. E. 2004. Man's Search for Meaning: The Classic Tribute to Hope from the Holocaust. London: Penguin Random House UK.

Hof, Enahm. 2023. "What Is the Wim Hof Method." Wim Hof Method. Accessed August 1, 2023. https://www.wimhofmethod.com/.

Hof, Wim. 2020. The Wim Hof Method—Activate Your Potential, Transcend Your Limits. London: Penguin Random House UK.

Nash, Tara. 2022. "Introducing Quantum Soul Coach, Christina de Stael." Conscious Grief. June 14, 2022. 18min 10sec. https://www.youtube.com/watch?v=qSMUuobxMxE&t=3s.

Touskova, Tereza Petraskova, Petr Bob, Zdenek Bares, Zdislava Vanickova, Daniel Nyvlt, and Jiri Raboch. 2022. "A Novel Wim Hof Psychophysiological Training Program to Reduce Stress Responses during an Antarctic Expedition." Journal of International Medical Research vol. 50, no. 4 (April 18, 2022). https://journals.sagepub.com/doi/10.1177/03000605221089883.

Van der Kolk, Bessel. 2014. The Body Keeps the Score: Brain, Mind, and Body in the Transformation of Trauma. London: Penguin Random House UK.

Yogapedia. 2020. Edmonton, Canada: Janalta. https://www.yogapedia.com/definition/4/yoga.

CHAPTER 7—MODERN MOURNING

Gilbert, Allison. 2016. Passed and Present: Keeping Memories of Loved Ones Alive. California: Seal Press.

Hale, Jennifer E. 2020. Have a Good Mourning: 17 Surprising Ways Loss Can Lead to Inspiration, Hope and Joy. USA: New Degree Press.

Klass, Dennis, Steven L. Nickman, and Phyllis R. Silverman. 1996. Continuing Bonds: New Understandings of Grief (Death Education, Aging and Health Care). New York: Routledge.

Nash, Tara. 2020. "When Peter Met Penny." The Chic Seeker (blog). October 8, 2020. https://thechicseeker.com/2020/10/08/when-peter-met-penny/.

Rando, Therese A. 1988. How to Go on Living When Someone You Love Dies. USA: Lexington Books.

Wolfelt, Dr. Alan D. 2020. "An Interview with Dr. Alan D. Wolfelt—Six Needs of Mourning." Marianne Gouveia. April 30, 2020. 59.38. https://www.youtube.com/watch?v=EOgoZrFWOQs.

CHAPTER 8—GIFTS OF CONSCIOUS GRIEF

Bates, Sasha. 2021. Languages of Loss: A Psychotherapist's Journey Through Grief. UK: Yellow Kite.

Brown, Brené. 2015. Daring Greatly: How the Courage to Be Vulnerable Transforms the Way We Live, Love, Parent, and Lead. New York: Avery.

Hannifin-MacNab, Susan. 2017. A to Z Healing Toolbox: A Practical Guide for Navigating Grief and Trauma with Intention. Minneapolis, Minnesota: Wise Ink Creative Publishing.

Hone, Dr. Lucy. 2019. "The Three Secrets of Resilient People." Filmed September 2019 in Christchurch New Zealand. TEDx video, 16.20. https://www.youtube.com/watch?v=NWH8N-BvhAw.

Oliver, Mary. 2006. Thirst: Poems by Mary Oliver. Boston: Beacon Press.

Rogers, Jane Duncan. 2015. Gifted by Grief: A True Story of Cancer, Loss and Rebirth. UK: Wild Wisdom Ltd.

CHAPTER 9—THE NEW YOU

Singer, Michael A. 2007. The Untethered Soul: The Journey Beyond Yourself. Oakland, California: New Harbinger Publications Inc.

The University of North Carolina Research Group. 2023. "What is PTG?" Post Traumatic Growth Research Group. August 14, 2023. https://ptgi.charlotte.edu/what-is-ptg/.

Wolfelt, Alan D., PhD. 2003. Understanding Your Grief: Ten Essential Touchstones for Finding Hope and Healing Your Heart. Fort Collins, Colorado: Companion Press.

HEART WORK

Printed in Great Britain
by Amazon

42325333R00116